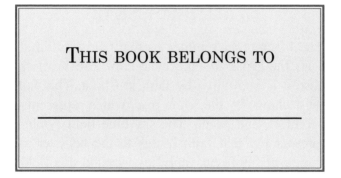

THIS BOOK BELONGS TO

_____

Luther's Seal

The black cross reminds us that Christ suffered and died on the cross to take away sin. The heart is red because it is kept alive by faith in Christ. This faith in Christ is shown by the white rose, which represents true joy, comfort, and peace. The sky blue field symbolizes the present joy that faith brings to the believer as the beginning of future heavenly joy. Around this field is a golden ring reminding us that heaven lasts forever and is more precious than any earthly treasure.

Luther's Small Catechism
and Explanation

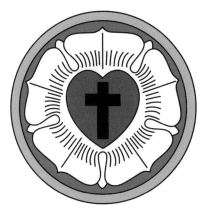

AMBASSADOR PUBLICATIONS
Minneapolis, Minnesota

©Copyright 2007
AMBASSADOR PUBLICATIONS
Board of Publications and Parish Education
Association of Free Lutheran Congregations

ISBN 978-1-58572-069-9
Library of Congress Control Number: 2007923208

PRINTED IN THE UNITED STATES OF AMERICA

TABLE OF CONTENTS

PREFACE

This current edition of *Luther's Small Catechism and Explanation* has been edited from the 1963 edition of *Luther's Small Catechism Explained.* Under the Board of Publications and Parish Education of the Association of Free Lutheran Congregations (AFLC), the 1963 edition was republished ten times, most recently in 1995. In preparing this new 2007 edition, the board carefully reviewed the 1963 edition, working under the guidance of the Coordinating Committee and AFLC Annual Conference.

Several updates have been made to the *Explanation*, which include

- P changing the Bible version of Scripture from the 1901 American Standard Version to New American Standard (1995 Updated Edition)
- P inserting a significant number of supplementary Scripture verses at the request of pastors
- P adding a brief biography of Martin Luther
- P adding reproductions of illustrated catechism posters in the *Luther's Small Catechism* section
- P adding an introduction to the *Explanation* section
- P incorporating all questions and answers from *Luther's Small Catechism* into *Sverdrup's Explanation* (for example, "Confession" between the Sacraments and "The Introduction" to the Lord's Prayer)
- P updating the format, including blue shaded boxes that set apart portions in the *Explanation* which are taken from *Luther's Small Catechism* (though slight variations may exist)
- P adding the three ecumenical creeds with historical introductions
- P revising and expanding the Glossary

Some language throughout the catechism has been updated for grammatical purposes or to clarify meaning. However, as in the past, the attempt has been made to communicate in the common language of the people so that all ages might benefit from the catechism. Where wording changes have been made, great care has been taken to preserve the integrity of the text, often consulting the Norwegian and German texts, as well as other English editions of the catechism.

Finally, the title has been changed from *Luther's Small Catechism Explained* to *Luther's Small Catechism and Explanation.* With the addition of "and Explanation" rather than merely "Explained," we hope to clearly indicate that our catechism is made up of two separate books—*Luther's Small Catechism* and *H. U. Sverdrup's Explanation.*

AFLC Board of Publications and Parish Education

Martin Luther: A Brief Biography

Who has had the greatest impact on our world during the past thousand years? At the turn of the twenty-first century, LIFE magazine picked Thomas Edison, the inventor of electricity, as number one, and Christopher Columbus, explorer of the New World, as number two. Third place was awarded to Martin Luther, the author of *The Small Catechism*. Who was this man, and why did his life have such an important impact on the world?

Born in 1483, Martin Luther was the oldest child of Hans and Margareta Luther, who lived in a region of Germany called Saxony. His father wanted him to be a lawyer, but a terrifying experience during a lightning storm led young Luther to become a Roman Catholic monk. His scholarly abilities later led to an appointment as professor at the new University of Wittenberg.

Pope Leo X, ruler of the Roman Catholic Church, sought to raise money for the completion of St. Peter's Church in Rome, and he authorized the sale of indulgences, letters of pardon which were believed to cancel punishment for sin and open the way from purgatory to heaven for those who purchased them.[1] The chief indulgence salesman, a monk named Johann Tetzel, made it sound like a person could buy the way to heaven, declaring "when the coin in the cash box rings, the soul from purgatory springs!"

On the day before All Saints Day 1517, Professor Luther, deeply troubled by this false teaching, posted a document called the *95 Theses* on the castle church door, which served as a campus bulletin board. Luther boldly wrote that salvation was received by repentance and trust in God's mercy, not by good works. Though his challenge to indulgences was probably intended for scholarly discussion, a firestorm of controversy was ignited as copies were quickly made and widely distributed.

It was through the study of the Bible that Luther finally came to assurance of salvation himself. While pondering Romans 1:17, he saw with new understanding that the righteousness of God is a gift to be received by faith. Many years later he recalled that he felt he was "altogether born again and had entered Paradise itself . . . ."[2]

Because powerful leaders of both church and state were angered by his writings, the monk from little Wittenberg was commanded to stand before the emperor and other officials when they gathered in the city of Worms in 1521. Given no chance to defend himself, Luther was shown a table piled high with material that he supposedly had written. "Are these your works? Do you take back what you have written?" he was asked. The next day he bravely replied:

> Unless I am convinced by the teachings of Holy Scripture or by sound reasoning . . . I am tied by the Scriptures I have quoted and by my conscience. I cannot and will not recant[3] anything, for to go against conscience is neither safe nor right. Here I stand. God help me! Amen.[4]

Some who heard him, including his own ruler, Frederick of Saxony, and other leaders, determined to stand with Luther. This beginning would eventually lead to the formation of the Lutheran Church and other Protestant denominations.

Luther was a university professor, but he always remained a pastor at heart. He was deeply concerned about the lack of basic Christian teachings among the people. This concern led him to prepare *The Small Catechism* in 1529, which was originally printed as large wall charts and later published as an illustrated booklet. His catechism included questions and answers on the Ten Commandments, the Apostles' Creed, the Lord's Prayer, and the Sacraments, together with suggested prayers for morning, evening, and mealtimes. Luther's primary desire was to equip Christian parents to lay a foundation of faith for their children. Only later would the catechism become a textbook for instruction of youth in the congregations.

Even after five hundred years, *Luther's Small Catechism* is still a timeless tool for teaching the fundamentals of the Christian faith in a way that is both doctrinal and devotional. It teaches about repentance, faith, and personal godliness and seeks to make knowledge a matter of the heart as well as the head.

Luther's pastor-heart is also revealed in the hymns that he wrote. Two of the most famous ones are "A Mighty Fortress Is Our God" and "Lord, Keep Us Steadfast in Your Word." He is especially remembered, too, for his translation of the Bible into the German language, making God's Word available to the common people.

Weary from his labors and in failing health, Luther journeyed to the city of his birth where his heart failed on February 18, 1546. As he was dying, there was comfort for him in repeating John 3:16. In his pocket afterwards was found a scrap of paper which read, "We are beggars. That is true."[5]

Martin Luther's work lives on as people read the Word of God which he labored to make available for everyone. His work lives on as the good news of salvation in Christ that he experienced and brought to light is heard. His work lives on as his hymns are sung and his catechism is studied. His work lives on as millions around the world today find a spiritual home in Lutheran congregations. Blessed be his memory!

Rev. Robert L. Lee

[1] Roman Catholics teach that purgatory is a place of suffering after death as a punishment for sins, preparing souls for heaven.

[2] Martin Luther, *Luther's Works*, eds. Jaroslav J. Pelikan and Helmut T. Lehmann, 55 vols. (St. Louis: Concordia Publishing House/Philadelphia: Fortress Press, 1955-1975), 25:xii.

[3] To recant is to publicly withdraw beliefs formerly held or statements made.

[4] Frederick Nohl, *Luther: Biography of a Reformer* (St. Louis: Concordia Publishing House, 2003), 107.

[5] Martin Luther, *Luther's Works*, eds. Jaroslav J. Pelikan and Helmut T. Lehmann, 55 vols. (St. Louis: Concordia Publishing House/Philadelphia: Fortress Press, 1955-1975), 54:476.

Suggested Reading:
Here I Stand by Roland Bainton
Luther the Reformer by James Kittelson
Luther: Biography of a Reformer by Frederick Nohl

Dr. Martin Luther's
SMALL CATECHISM
1529

Intersynodical Translation
Adopted by
The Lutheran Free Church
1929

Updated by
AFLC Board of Publications
and Parish Education
2007

AMBASSADOR PUBLICATIONS
Minneapolis, Minnesota

I am the LORD thy God.

I

Thou shalt have no other gods before Me.

II

Thou shalt not take the name of the LORD thy God in vain, for the LORD will not hold him guiltless that taketh His name in vain.

III

Remember the Sabbath day, to keep it holy.

IV

Honor thy father and thy mother, that thy days may be long upon the land which the LORD thy God giveth thee.

V

Thou shalt not kill.

VI

Thou shalt not commit adultery.

VII

Thou shalt not steal.

VIII

Thou shalt not bear false witness against thy neighbor.

IX

Thou shalt not covet thy neighbor's house.

X

Thou shalt not covet thy neighbor's wife, nor his manservant, nor his maidservant, nor his cattle, nor anything that is thy neighbor's.

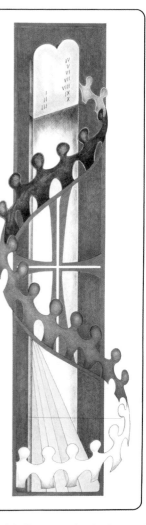

"The Commandments teach a man to know his illness, so that he feels and sees what he can do and what he cannot leave undone, and thus knows himself to be a sinner and a wicked man."

— Martin Luther

PART I

THE TEN COMMANDMENTS

THE INTRODUCTION

I am the LORD thy God.

THE FIRST COMMANDMENT

Thou shalt have no other gods before Me.

What does this mean?

We should fear, love, and trust in God above all things.

THE SECOND COMMANDMENT

Thou shalt not take the Name of the LORD thy God in vain; for the LORD will not hold him guiltless that taketh His Name in vain.

What does this mean?

We should fear and love God so that we do not curse, swear, conjure, lie, or deceive, by His Name, but call upon Him in every time of need and worship Him with prayer, praise, and thanksgiving.

The Third Commandment

Remember the Sabbath day, to keep it holy.

What does this mean?

We should fear and love God so that we do not despise His Word and the preaching of the same, but regard it as holy and gladly hear and learn it.

The Fourth Commandment

Honor thy father and thy mother, that thy days may be long upon the land which the Lord thy God giveth thee.

What does this mean?

We should fear and love God so that we do not despise our parents and superiors, nor provoke them to anger, but honor, serve, obey, love, and respect them.

The Fifth Commandment

Thou shalt not kill.

What does this mean?

We should fear and love God so that we do our neighbor no bodily harm nor cause him any suffering, but help and befriend him in every need.

THE SIXTH COMMANDMENT

Thou shalt not commit adultery.

What does this mean?

We should fear and love God so that we lead a chaste and pure life in word and deed, and that husband and wife love and honor each other.

THE SEVENTH COMMANDMENT

Thou shalt not steal.

What does this mean?

We should fear and love God so that we do not rob our neighbor of his money or property, nor bring them into our possession by unfair dealing or fraud, but help him to improve and protect his property and living.

THE EIGHTH COMMANDMENT

Thou shalt not bear false witness against thy neighbor.

What does this mean?

We should fear and love God so that we do not deceitfully lie about, betray, backbite, nor slander our neighbor, but defend him, speak well of him, and put the most charitable construction on all that he does.

THE NINTH COMMANDMENT

Thou shalt not covet thy neighbor's house.

What does this mean?

We should fear and love God so that we do not seek by craftiness to gain possession of our neighbor's inheritance or home, nor obtain them under pretense of a legal right, but assist and serve him in keeping the same.

THE TENTH COMMANDMENT

Thou shalt not covet thy neighbor's wife, nor his manservant, nor his maidservant, nor his cattle, nor anything that is thy neighbor's.

What does this mean?

We should fear and love God so that we do not estrange or entice away our neighbor's wife, servants, or cattle, but seek to have them remain and fulfill their duty to him.

THE CONCLUSION

What does God say of all these Commandments?

I the LORD thy God am a jealous God, visiting the iniquity of the fathers upon the children unto the third and fourth generation of them that hate Me; and showing mercy unto thousands of them that love Me and keep My commandments.

What does this mean?

God threatens to punish all who transgress these commandments.
We should, therefore, fear His wrath, and in no way disobey them.
But He promises grace and every blessing to all who keep them. We
should, therefore, love Him, trust in Him, and gladly keep His
commandments.

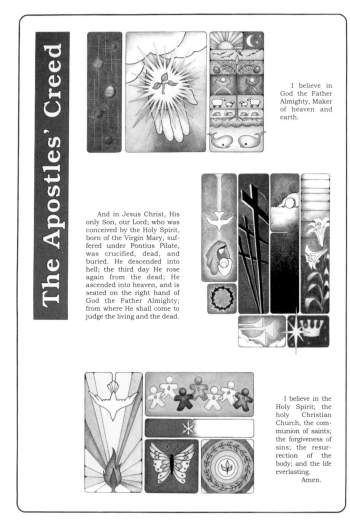

The Apostles' Creed

I believe in God the Father Almighty, Maker of heaven and earth.

And in Jesus Christ, His only Son, our Lord; who was conceived by the Holy Spirit, born of the Virgin Mary, suffered under Pontius Pilate, was crucified, dead, and buried. He descended into hell; the third day He rose again from the dead; He ascended into heaven, and is seated on the right hand of God the Father Almighty; from where He shall come to judge the living and the dead.

I believe in the Holy Spirit; the holy Christian Church, the communion of saints; the forgiveness of sins; the resurrection of the body; and the life everlasting.
Amen.

"The Creed shows [man] and teaches him where he may find the remedy—the grace which helps him to become a good man and to keep the Commandments; it shows him God, and the mercy which He has revealed and offered in Christ."

— Martin Luther

PART II

THE APOSTLES' CREED

THE FIRST ARTICLE
OF CREATION

I believe in God the Father Almighty, Maker of heaven and earth.

What does this mean?

I believe that God has created me and all that exists; that He has given and still preserves to me my body and soul, my eyes and ears, and all my members, my reason and all the powers of my soul, together with food and clothing, home and family, and all my property; that He daily provides abundantly for all the needs of my life, protects me from all danger, and guards and keeps me from all evil; and that He does this purely out of fatherly and divine goodness and mercy, without any merit or worthiness in me; for all of which I am in duty bound to thank, praise, serve, and obey Him. This is most certainly true.

THE SECOND ARTICLE
OF REDEMPTION

And in Jesus Christ His only Son, our Lord; Who was conceived by the Holy Spirit, Born of the Virgin Mary; Suffered under Pontius Pilate, Was crucified, dead, and buried; He descended into hell; The third day He rose again from the dead; He ascended into heaven, And is seated on the right hand of God the Father Almighty; From where He shall come to judge the living and the dead.

What does this mean?

I believe that Jesus Christ, true God, begotten of the Father from eternity, and also true Man, born of the Virgin Mary, is my Lord; who has redeemed me, a lost and condemned creature, bought me and freed me from all sins, from death, and from the power of the devil; not with silver and gold, but with His holy and precious blood and with His innocent sufferings and death; in order that I might be His own, live under Him in His kingdom, and serve Him in everlasting righteousness, innocence, and blessedness; even as He is risen from the dead and lives and reigns to all eternity. This is most certainly true.

THE THIRD ARTICLE
OF SANCTIFICATION

I believe in the Holy Spirit; The holy Christian Church, The Communion of Saints; The Forgiveness of sins; The Resurrection of the body; And the Life everlasting. Amen.

What does this mean?

I believe that I cannot by my own reason or strength believe in Jesus Christ my Lord or come to Him; but the Holy Spirit has called me through the Gospel, enlightened me with His gifts, and sanctified and preserved me in the true faith; in like manner as He calls, gathers, enlightens, and sanctifies the whole Christian Church on earth, and preserves it in union with Jesus Christ in the one true faith; in this Christian Church, He daily forgives abundantly all my sins and the sins of all believers, and at the last day will raise up me and all the dead and will grant everlasting life to me and to all who believe in Christ. This is most certainly true.

The Lord's Prayer

Our Father who art in heaven,

Hallowed be Thy name.
Thy kingdom come.
Thy will be done on
earth, as it is in heaven.
Give us this day our
daily bread.
And forgive us our
trespasses, as we
forgive those who
trespass against us.
And lead us not into
temptation,
but deliver us from evil.

For Thine is the kingdom,
and the power, and the glory,
for ever and ever.   Amen.

"The Lord's Prayer teaches [man] how to ask for this grace, get it, and take it to himself, to wit, by habitual, humble, comforting prayer; then grace is given, and by the fulfillment of God's commandments he is saved."

— Martin Luther

PART III

THE LORD'S PRAYER

THE INTRODUCTION

Our Father, who art in heaven.

What does this mean?

God thereby tenderly encourages us to believe that He is truly our Father and that we are truly His children, so that we may boldly and confidently come to Him in prayer, even as beloved children come to their dear father.

THE FIRST PETITION

Hallowed be Thy Name.

What does this mean?

God's Name is indeed holy in itself, but we pray in this petition that it may be hallowed also among us.

How is this done?

When the Word of God is taught in its truth and purity, and we as God's children lead holy lives in accordance with it. This grant us, dear Father in heaven! But whoever teaches and lives otherwise than God's Word teaches profanes the Name of God among us. From this preserve us, heavenly Father!

THE SECOND PETITION

Thy kingdom come.

What does this mean?

The kingdom of God comes indeed of itself without our prayer, but we pray in this petition that it may come also to us.

How is this done?

When our heavenly Father gives us His Holy Spirit, so that by His grace we believe His holy Word and live a godly life here on earth and in heaven forever.

THE THIRD PETITION

Thy will be done, on earth as it is in heaven.

What does this mean?

The good and gracious will of God is done indeed without our prayer, but we pray in this petition that it may be done also among us.

How is this done?

When God destroys and brings to nothing every evil counsel and purpose of the devil, the world, and our own flesh, which would hinder us from hallowing His Name and prevent the coming of His kingdom; and when He strengthens us and keeps us steadfast in His Word and in faith, even unto our end. This is His good and gracious will.

THE FOURTH PETITION

Give us this day our daily bread.

What does this mean?

God indeed gives daily bread to all men, even to the wicked, without our prayer; but we pray in this petition that He would lead us to acknowledge our daily bread as His gift and to receive it with thanksgiving.

What is meant by daily bread?

Everything that is required to satisfy our bodily needs such as food and clothing, house and home, fields and flocks, money and goods; pious parents, children, and servants; godly and faithful rulers, good government; seasonable weather, peace and health; order and honor; true friends, good neighbors, and the like.

THE FIFTH PETITION

And forgive us our trespasses, as we forgive those who trespass against us.

What does this mean?

We pray in this petition that our heavenly Father would not regard our sins nor because of them deny our prayers; for we neither merit nor are worthy of those things for which we pray; but that He would grant us all things through grace, even though we sin daily and deserve nothing but punishment. And certainly we, on our part, will heartily forgive and gladly do good to those who may sin against us.

The Sixth Petition

And lead us not into temptation.

What does this mean?

God indeed tempts no one to sin; but we pray in this petition that God would so guard and preserve us that the devil, the world, and our own flesh may not deceive us nor lead us into error and unbelief, despair, and other great and shameful sins; but that when so tempted, we may finally prevail and gain the victory.

The Seventh Petition

But deliver us from evil.

What does this mean?

We pray in this petition, in summary, that our heavenly Father would deliver us from all manner of evil, whether it affect body or soul, property or reputation, and at last, when the hour of death shall come, grant us a blessed end and graciously take us from this world of sorrow to Himself in heaven.

THE CONCLUSION

For Thine is the kingdom, and the power, and the glory, for ever and ever. Amen.

What does the word "Amen" mean?

It means that I should be assured that these petitions are acceptable to our heavenly Father and are heard by Him; for He Himself has commanded us to pray in this manner and has promised to hear us. Amen, Amen, that is, Yes, Yes, it shall be so.

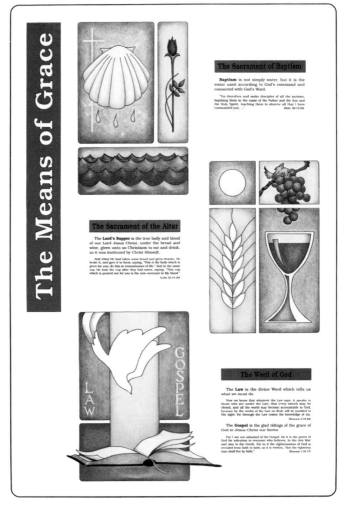

The Means of Grace

The Sacrament of Baptism

Baptism is not simply water, but it is the water used according to God's command and connected with God's Word.

"Go therefore and make disciples of all the nations, baptizing them in the name of the Father and the Son and the Holy Spirit, teaching them to observe all that I have commanded you, ..."

Matt. 28:19-20

The Sacrament of the Altar

The **Lord's Supper** is the true body and blood of our Lord Jesus Christ, under the bread and wine, given unto us Christians to eat and drink, as it was instituted by Christ Himself.

And when He had taken some bread and given thanks, He broke it, and gave it to them, saying, "This is My body which is given for you; do this in remembrance of Me." And in the same way He took the cup after they had eaten, saying, "This cup which is poured out for you is the new covenant in My blood."

Luke 22:19-20

The Word of God

The **Law** is the divine Word which tells us what we must do.

Now we know that whatever the Law says, it speaks to those who are under the Law, that every mouth may be closed, and all the world may become accountable to God; because by the works of the Law no flesh will be justified in His sight; for through the Law comes the knowledge of sin.

Romans 3:19-20

The **Gospel** is the glad tidings of the grace of God in Jesus Christ our Savior.

For I am not ashamed of the Gospel, for it is the power of God for salvation to everyone who believes, to the Jew first and also to the Greek. For in it the righteousness of God is revealed from faith to faith; as it is written, "But the righteous man shall live by faith."

Romans 1:16-17

"The Word itself, Baptism, and the Lord's Supper are our morning stars to which we turn our eyes as certain indications of the Sun of grace. For we can definitely assert that where the Lord's Supper, Baptism, and the Word are found, Christ, the remission of sins, and life eternal are found."

— Martin Luther

PART IV

THE SACRAMENT OF BAPTISM

I
WHAT IS BAPTISM?

Baptism is not simply water, but it is the water used according to God's command and connected with God's Word.

What is this word of God?

It is the word of our Lord Jesus Christ, as recorded in the last chapter of Matthew: "Go therefore and make disciples of all the nations, baptizing them in the name of the Father and the Son and the Holy Spirit."

II
WHAT GIFTS OR BENEFITS DOES BAPTISM BESTOW?

Baptism works forgiveness of sins, delivers from death and the devil, and gives everlasting salvation to all who believe, as the word and promise of God declare.

What is this word and promise of God?

It is the word of our Lord Jesus Christ, as recorded in the last chapter of Mark: "He who has believed and has been baptized shall be saved; but he who has disbelieved shall be condemned."

III
HOW CAN WATER DO SUCH GREAT THINGS?

It is not the water, indeed, that does such great things, but the Word of God, connected with the water, and our faith which relies on that Word of God. For without the Word of God, it is simply water and no baptism. But when connected with the Word of God, it is a baptism, that is, a gracious water of life and a washing of regeneration in the Holy Spirit, as St. Paul says to Titus, in the third chapter: "He saved us, not on the basis of deeds which we have done in righteousness, but according to His mercy, by the washing of regeneration and renewing by the Holy Spirit, whom He poured out upon us richly through Jesus Christ our Savior; so that being justified by His grace we would be made heirs according to the hope of eternal life. This is a trustworthy statement."

IV
WHAT DOES SUCH BAPTIZING WITH WATER SIGNIFY?

It signifies that the old Adam in us, together with all sins and evil lusts, should be drowned by daily sorrow and repentance and be put to death; and that the new man should daily come forth and rise to live before God in righteousness and holiness forever.

Where is it so written?

St. Paul writes in the sixth chapter of the Epistle to the Romans: "Therefore we have been buried with Him through baptism into death, so that as Christ was raised from the dead through the glory of the Father, so we too might walk in newness of life."

CONFESSION

What is Confession?

Confession consists of two parts: the one is that we confess our sins; the other, that we receive absolution or forgiveness from the pastor as from God Himself, in no way doubting, but firmly believing that our sins are thereby forgiven before God in heaven.

What sins should we confess?

Before God we should acknowledge ourselves guilty of all manner of sins, even those of which we are not aware, as we do in the Lord's Prayer. To the pastor we should confess only those sins which we know and feel in our hearts.

What are such sins?

Here examine yourself in the light of the Ten Commandments, whether as father or mother, son or daughter, master or servant, you have been disobedient, unfaithful, slothful, ill-tempered, unchaste, or quarrelsome, or whether you have injured anyone by word or deed, stolen, neglected or wasted anything, or done any other evil.

PART V

THE SACRAMENT OF THE ALTAR

I
WHAT IS THE SACRAMENT OF THE ALTAR?

It is the true Body and Blood of our Lord Jesus Christ, under the bread and wine, given unto us Christians to eat and to drink, as it was instituted by Christ Himself.

Where is it so written?

The holy Evangelists, Matthew, Mark, and Luke, together with St. Paul, write:

"Our Lord Jesus Christ, in the night in which He was betrayed, took bread; and when He had given thanks, He broke it and gave it to His disciples saying, 'Take, eat; this is My Body, which is given for you; this do in remembrance of Me.'

"In the same manner, also, when He had eaten, He took the cup, and when He had given thanks, He gave it to them saying, 'Drink of it, all of you; this cup is the New Testament in My Blood, which is shed for you, and for many, for the forgiveness of sins; this do, as often as you drink it, in remembrance of Me.'"

II
WHAT IS THE BENEFIT OF SUCH EATING AND DRINKING?

It is pointed out in these words: "Given and shed for you for the forgiveness of sins." Through these words, the forgiveness of sins, life and salvation are given unto us in the Sacrament. For where there is forgiveness of sins, there is also life and salvation.

III
HOW CAN THE BODILY EATING AND DRINKING PRODUCE SUCH GREAT BENEFITS?

The eating and drinking, indeed, do not produce them, but the words: "Given and shed for you for the forgiveness of sins." For besides the bodily eating and drinking, these words are the chief thing in the Sacrament; and anyone who believes them has what they say and declare, namely, the forgiveness of sins.

IV
WHO, THEN, RECEIVES THIS SACRAMENT WORTHILY?

Fasting and bodily preparation are indeed a good outward discipline, but that person is truly worthy and well prepared who believes these words: "Given and shed for you for the forgiveness of sins." But anyone who does not believe these words or who doubts them is unworthy and unprepared, for the words "for you" require truly believing hearts.

LUTHER'S PRAYERS

MORNING PRAYER

I thank You, my heavenly Father, through Jesus Christ, Your dear Son, that You have kept me through the night from all harm and danger. I pray that You would keep me this day from all sin and evil, that in all my thoughts and words and deeds I may serve and please You. Into Your hands I commend my body and soul and all that is mine. Let Your holy angels be with me, that the evil one may have no power over me. This I pray in Jesus' name. Amen.

EVENING PRAYER

I thank You, my heavenly Father, through Jesus Christ, Your dear Son, that You have graciously kept me through this day. I pray that You would forgive me all my sin and the wrong that I have done. By Your great mercy, keep me this night from all harm and danger. Into Your hands I commend my body and soul and all that is mine. Let Your holy angels be with me, that the evil one may have no power over me. This I pray in Jesus' name. Amen.

BLESSING BEFORE MEALS

The eyes of all wait upon thee, O Lord, and thou givest them their meat in due season. Thou openest thine hand and satisfiest the desire of every living thing. Amen. (*from Psalm 145:15-16 KJV*)

Lord God, heavenly Father, bless us and these Your gifts which we receive from Your bountiful goodness, through Jesus Christ our Lord. Amen.

THANKSGIVING AFTER MEALS

O give thanks unto the Lord, for He is good; for his mercy endureth for ever. Amen. (*from Psalm 106:1 KJV*)

Lord God, heavenly Father, we thank You for all Your gifts, through Jesus Christ our Lord, who lives and reigns forever. Amen.

H. U. Sverdrup's
Explanation
of
Luther's
Small Catechism

By
HARALD ULRICH SVERDRUP 1864

ABRIDGED 1897

Translated from the Norwegian by
HANS A. URSETH 1900

Revised by Rev. John A. Houkom 1929

Republished by AFLC Board of Publications
and Parish Education 1963

Revised and updated by AFLC Board of Publications
and Parish Education 2007

Ambassador Publications
Minneapolis, Minnesota

An Introduction
to the Explanation of Our Catechism

Dr. Martin Luther's Small Catechism, written by Martin Luther in 1529, is only the first section of our catechism book. The larger section, called *H. U. Sverdrup's Explanation*, develops the topics in the catechism with questions, answers, and Bible references.

This *Explanation* is condensed from a book entitled *Truth Unto Godliness*, which was prepared in 1737 by a chaplain to the king of Denmark and Norway named Erik Pontoppidan. He would later become the bishop of Bergen. His model was a similar book called *A Simple Explanation of Christian Teaching*, written in 1677 by Philip J. Spener, father of the spiritual life movement in Germany known as Lutheran pietism.

Containing 759 questions and answers, Pontopiddan's explanation became the exclusive religious text in Norway for nearly one hundred and fifty years. In fact, the main purpose of the public school system in Norway, established in 1739, was to teach children to read and write so that they could study the explanation and prepare for confirmation. It would be hard to think of any book, other than the Bible itself, that has so profoundly influenced the life of a nation.

A Norwegian Lutheran pastor, Harald U. Sverdrup, completed the task of updating and shortening Pontopiddan's explanation in 1864. Sverdrup "did not permit any other form of faith than the Holy Scripture, no tradition, no oral Word, and this fundamental view is followed consistently. It is marked both by simple faith and clear thinking."[1] It is interesting to note that H. U. Sverdrup was the father of Professor Georg Sverdrup, one of the founders of the Lutheran Free Church in the United States in 1897.

Our catechism includes a slightly altered English edition of the elder Sverdrup's work, translated in 1900 by Hans A. Urseth, a professor of theology at Augsburg Seminary, Minneapolis, Minnesota.

It was later slightly revised in 1929 by another Lutheran Free
Church pastor, John A. Houkom.

In 1962-63 when the Lutheran Free Church merged with The
American Lutheran Church (TALC), the congregations that chose
not to join TALC formed the Association of Free Lutheran
Congregations. These congregations continued republishing the
Lutheran Free Church catechism under the AFLC Board of
Publications and Parish Education until this present revised edition.

Rev. Robert L. Lee

---

[1] Andreas Helland, *Georg Sverdrup: The Man and His Message* (Minneapolis: Messenger
Press, 1947), 16.

PREFACE TO THE REVISED EDITION [1929]

In his preface to his translation of *Luther's Small Catechism Explained* which appeared in 1900, Prof. H. A. Urseth said:

> In 1897 the present publishers issued in Norwegian an Explanation of Luther's Small Catechism by Pastor H. U. Sverdrup, being an abridged edition of a larger work by the same author, based on Dr. Pontoppidan's Explanation of the Catechism. Some alterations were made in answers 243-252. The present work is a translation of this abridged and slightly altered edition.
>
> A literal translation has been avoided rather than sought; an attempt has been made to render the original in the simplest and strongest English, and to avoid words and expressions with which the young are little familiar.
>
> *   *   *
>
> Scripture quotations have been added somewhat freely from the larger edition.
>
> As the needs of our English speaking young people have been constantly borne in mind during the preparation of this translation, it is hoped that the book may not fail to carry some blessing to them.

In the present revised edition, the **Intersynodical Translation** of Luther's Small Catechism, adopted by the Lutheran Free Church Annual Conference in 1929, has been incorporated, and necessary alterations in the text of this work have been made to conform therewith. Also, the text of the American Standard Version of the Bible has replaced the versions used in the Scripture quotations throughout the original edition.

John A. Houkom

INTRODUCTION

1. **What is God's will concerning man?**
   God wills that all men should be saved and come to the knowledge of the truth. I Timothy 2:4

2. **Where does God show us how we may be saved?**
   In the holy Scriptures, also called the Bible.

   > **I Peter 1:23** For you have been born again not of seed which is perishable but imperishable, *that is*, through the living and enduring word of God.

3. **Who wrote the Bible?**
   The holy prophets, evangelists, and apostles wrote the Bible.

4. **But how can their word be the Word of God?**
   The Spirit of God revealed to them what to speak and write.

   > **II Peter 1:20-21** But know this first of all, that no prophecy of Scripture is *a matter* of one's own interpretation, for no prophecy was ever made by an act of human will, but men moved by the Holy Spirit spoke from God.

5. **What must we do to experience personally that their word is the Word of God?**
   We must obey the Word and receive it into our hearts.

   > **Psalm 119:11** Your word I have treasured in my heart, that I may not sin against You.

6. **Is the Bible then the only safe rule of our faith and duty?**
   Yes; the Bible alone contains full information of the will of God concerning our salvation.

   > **II Timothy 3:15** And that from childhood you have known the sacred

writings which are able to give you the wisdom that leads to salvation
through faith which is in Christ Jesus.

7. **How do we rightly use the Word of God?**
   We must first look to God for the enlightenment of His Spirit
   and then read the Word with devotion and an earnest purpose
   to live according to it.

   > **I Corinthians 2:14** But a natural man does not accept the things of the
   > Spirit of God, for they are foolishness to him; and he cannot understand
   > them, because they are spiritually appraised.
   > **Acts 17:11b** For they received the word with great eagerness,
   > examining the Scriptures daily *to see* whether these things were so.
   > **Joshua 1:8b** "But you shall meditate on it day and night, so that you
   > may be careful to do according to all that is written in it."

8. **Who should read the Bible?**
   It is the will of God that all should use His Word and love it
   as a dear gift.

9. **What is the central truth of all the books of the Bible?**
   The great truth that Jesus is the way to salvation for all who
   believe.

   > **John 20:31** But these have been written so that you may believe that
   > Jesus is the Christ, the Son of God; and that believing you may have life
   > in His name.
   > **John 14:6** Jesus said to him, "I am the way, and the truth, and the life;
   > no one comes to the Father but through Me."

10. **How is the Bible divided in regard to its teaching?**
    It is divided into Law and Gospel.

11. **What is the Law?**
    The Law is the divine Word which tells us what we must do.

    > **Galatians 3:10b** "CURSED IS EVERYONE WHO DOES NOT ABIDE BY ALL
    > THINGS WRITTEN IN THE BOOK OF THE LAW, TO PERFORM THEM."

Joshua 22:5 "Only be very careful to observe the commandment and the law which Moses the servant of the LORD commanded you, to love the LORD your God and walk in all His ways and keep His commandments and hold fast to Him and serve Him with all your heart and with all your soul."

12. What is the Gospel?

The Gospel is the good news of the grace of God in Jesus Christ our Savior.

John 3:16 "For God so loved the world, that He gave His only begotten Son, that whoever believes in Him shall not perish, but have eternal life."

II Corinthians 5:21 He made Him who knew no sin *to be* sin on our behalf, so that we might become the righteousness of God in Him.

PART ONE

THE TEN COMMANDMENTS, OR THE LAW

13. How has God given His Law to us?
1. In the Creation God wrote His Law in the heart of man. (Conscience) Romans 2:15
2. At Mount Sinai He gave His Law in the Ten Commandments, written on two tables of stone. Exodus 20:1-17

14. Does this Law demand outward observance only?
No; it demands the whole man and the willing obedience of heart and mind.

> **Luke 10:27** "YOU SHALL LOVE THE LORD YOUR GOD WITH ALL YOUR HEART, AND WITH ALL YOUR SOUL, AND WITH ALL YOUR STRENGTH, AND WITH ALL YOUR MIND; AND YOUR NEIGHBOR AS YOURSELF."

15. Can we be saved through the Law?
No; since the fall in sin, no man can perfectly keep the Law.

> **Romans 8:7** The mind set on the flesh is hostile toward God; for it does not subject itself to the law of God, for it is not even able *to do so*.
> **Romans 3:20** By the works of the Law no flesh will be justified in His sight; for through the Law *comes* the knowledge of sin.

16. Of what benefit, then, is the Law?
1. It points out to us our sins and the wrath of God toward sin.

> **Romans 3:20b** For through the Law *comes* the knowledge of sin.

2. It makes us anxious to seek Christ.

> **Galatians 3:24a** The Law has become our tutor *to lead us* to Christ.

3. It points out to the believer what fruits his faith must bear.

> **Psalm 119:105** Your word is a lamp to my feet and a light to my path.

17. What is the substance of the Law?
Love to God, ourselves, and our neighbor. Matthew 22:37-40

> **Romans 13:10b** Love is the fulfillment of *the* law.
> **I Timothy 1:5a** But the goal of our instruction is love from a pure heart.

THE FIRST TABLE OF THE LAW

18. What is the substance of the first table?
Love to God.

> **Luke 10:27a** "YOU SHALL LOVE THE LORD YOUR GOD WITH ALL YOUR HEART, AND WITH ALL YOUR SOUL, AND WITH ALL YOUR STRENGTH, AND WITH ALL YOUR MIND."

THE FIRST COMMANDMENT

Thou shalt have no other gods before Me.

What does this mean?

We should fear, love, and trust in God above all things.

---

19. **What does the first commandment forbid?**
    It forbids the worship of false gods or idols.

    > **Matthew 4:10b** "'YOU SHALL WORSHIP THE LORD YOUR GOD, AND SERVE HIM ONLY.'"
    > **I John 5:21** Little children, guard yourselves from idols.

20. **What is meant by an idol?**
    Anything that man worships, fears, loves, and trusts instead of the one true God.

21. **Who practice idolatry openly?**
    They who worship the created things instead of the Creator and pray to the sun, the moon, stars, images, angels, or saints.

    > **Romans 1:25** For they exchanged the truth of God for a lie, and worshiped and served the creature rather than the Creator, who is blessed forever. Amen.
    > **Deuteronomy 4:15-19**

22. **Who practice idolatry secretly?**
    They who turn their love, fear, and trust from the living God, that they may secretly cling to something other than Him.

    > **Matthew 10:37** "He who loves father or mother more than Me is not worthy of Me; and he who loves son or daughter more than Me is not worthy of Me."
    > **I Timothy 6:10a** For the love of money is a root of all sorts of evil.

23. **Whom do all idolaters really serve?**
    They serve the devil, who is the father of lies and the lord of all impenitent and hardened sinners.

    > **I John 3:8a** The one who practices sin is of the devil.
    > **II Corinthians 4:4a** The god of this world has blinded the minds of the unbelieving.

24. **What does God require of us in the first commandment?**
    We should fear, love, and trust in God above all things.

    > **Matthew 4:10b** "'You shall worship the Lord your God, and serve Him only.'"

25. **Upon what does God then really look?**
    Upon the attitude of our hearts toward Him.

    > **I Samuel 16:7b** "For God *sees* not as man sees, for man looks at the outward appearance, but the Lord looks at the heart."
    > **Proverbs 4:23** Watch over your heart with all diligence, for from it *flow* the springs of life.

26. **When do we fear God?**
    We fear God when we think so highly of Him that we are afraid of offending Him by any wrongdoing.

    > **Psalm 33:8** Let all the earth fear the Lord; let all the inhabitants of the world stand in awe of Him.

27. **Of how many kinds is the fear of God?**
    Of two kinds: slavish fear and childlike fear.

28. **What is meant by slavish fear?**
    When we fear God because we are afraid of punishment.

    > **Luke 12:5** "But I will warn you whom to fear: fear the One who, after He has killed, has authority to cast into hell; yes, I tell you, fear Him!"

29. **What is meant by childlike fear?**
    When we love God so dearly that we wish to do nothing that is against His will.

    > **Genesis 39:9b** "How then could I do this great evil and sin against God?"
    > **I John 4:18b** Perfect love casts out fear.

30. Who fear God in this manner?

God's children only.

> **Romans 8:15** For you have not received a spirit of slavery leading to fear again, but you have received a spirit of adoption as sons by which we cry out, "Abba! Father!"

31. When do we love God?

We love God when He is dearer to us than all else, so that we have no true joy except in Him and gladly submit to His will in all things.

> **Psalm 18:1** "I love You, O LORD, my strength."
> **Psalm 73:25-26** Whom have I in heaven *but You?* And besides You, I desire nothing on earth. My flesh and my heart may fail, but God is the strength of my heart and my portion forever.

32. Can we love God and the world at the same time?

By no means.

> **Matthew 6:24** "No one can serve two masters; for either he will hate the one and love the other, or he will be devoted to one and despise the other. You cannot serve God and wealth."
> **I John 2:15** Do not love the world nor the things in the world. If anyone loves the world, the love of the Father is not in him.

33. Why must we love God?

We must love God because of His goodness toward us.

> **Matthew 19:17b** "There is *only* One who is good."
> **I John 4:19** We love, because He first loved us.

34. How do we show love for God?

By a holy life.

> **John 14:21a** "He who has My commandments and keeps them is the one who loves Me."

35. When do we trust in God above all things?

We trust in God above all things when we have confidence in Him as in a loving father, and when we look to Him for every blessing and put all our affairs into His hands.

> **I Peter 5:7** Casting all your anxiety on Him, because He cares for you.
> **Psalm 37:5** Commit your way to the Lord, trust also in Him, and He will do it.

36. Why must we trust in God alone?

Because He is our almighty and faithful Friend.

> **Psalm 4:8** In peace I will both lie down and sleep, for You alone, O Lord, make me to dwell in safety.

37. Name some virtues that result from true fear, love, and trust in God.

Humility, patience, and self-denial.

> **I Peter 5:5b-6** For God is opposed to the proud, but gives grace to the humble. Therefore humble yourselves under the mighty hand of God, that He may exalt you at the proper time.
> **Job 1:21b** "The Lord gave and the Lord has taken away. Blessed be the name of the Lord."
> **Matthew 26:39c** "Yet not as I will, but as You will."

THE SECOND COMMANDMENT

Thou shalt not take the Name of the LORD thy God in vain; for the LORD will not hold him guiltless that taketh His Name in vain.

What does this mean?

We should fear and love God so that we do not curse, swear, conjure, lie, or deceive, by His Name, but call upon Him in every time of need and worship Him with prayer, praise, and thanksgiving.

---

38. **What is meant by the "name" of God?**
    1. The usual names given to Him in the Bible.
    2. His nature and attributes and all by which He is especially known, such as His Word, sacraments, and works.

       Psalm 8:1 O LORD, our Lord, how majestic is Your name in all the earth, who have displayed Your splendor above the heavens!

39. **When is the name of God taken in vain?**
    When it is used in a thoughtless and mocking manner and without devotion and reverence.

40. **How is this done?**
    1. When we use God's name or Word in jesting or as a byword.
    2. When we find fault with anything God has done.
    3. When we use the name of God in cursing, swearing, conjuring, lying, or deceiving.

41. **What is it to curse by the name of God?**
It is to call down evil by the name of God upon ourselves,
our neighbor, or any other created thing.

42. **What is it to swear by the name of God?**
It is to bear witness to anything by the holy name of God.

43. **Are we ever permitted to swear?**
Yes; when the proper authorities demand it; for example,
testimony in court, oath of office, and marriage vows.

44. **Why is it a great sin to commit perjury?**
Because the perjurer shows open disregard for God and the
salvation of his own soul and frankly calls down the
judgment of God upon himself.

> **Colossians 3:9** Do not lie to one another, since you laid aside the old
> self with its *evil* practices.

45. **Are cursing and swearing sinful when the name of God is
not used?**
Yes, indeed; for whatever we curse or swear by, we really do
so by God, who is the Lord of all things.

> **Matthew 5:34-37** "But I say to you, make no oath at all, either by
> heaven, for it is the throne of God, or by the earth, for it is the footstool
> of His feet, or by Jerusalem, for it is THE CITY OF THE GREAT KING. Nor
> shall you make an oath by your head, for you cannot make one hair
> white or black. But let your statement be, 'Yes, yes' *or* 'No, no';
> anything beyond these is of evil."
> **Ephesians 4:29** Let no unwholesome word proceed from your mouth,
> but only such *a word* as is good for edification according to the need *of
> the moment*, so that it will give grace to those who hear.

46. **Are cursing and swearing sinful when they have become a
habit?**
Most certainly; for a sinful habit proves that sin is our master.

47. What is it to conjure by the name of God?
It is practicing magic, witchcraft, or any other kind of superstition, using the name of God or a passage from the Bible.

> **Deuteronomy 18:10-12**

48. How do we lie and deceive by the name of God?
By perjury, false teaching, and hypocrisy.

> **Matthew 15:9** "'BUT IN VAIN DO THEY WORSHIP ME, TEACHING AS DOCTRINES THE PRECEPTS OF MEN.'"
> **Titus 1:16a** They profess to know God, but by *their* deeds they deny *Him.*

49. What must he expect who takes the name of God in vain?
Great punishment, both in time and eternity; for the Lord will not hold him guiltless who takes His name in vain. Exodus 20:7

> **Matthew 12:36** "But I tell you that every careless word that people speak, they shall give an accounting for it in the day of judgment."

50. How do we use the name of God properly?
When we sincerely call upon Him in every time of need and worship Him with prayer, praise, and thanksgiving.

> **Psalm 103:1** Bless the LORD, O my soul, and all that is within me, *bless* His holy name.

The Third Commandment

Remember the Sabbath day, to keep it holy.

What does this mean?

We should fear and love God so that we do not despise His Word and the preaching of the same, but regard it as holy and gladly hear and learn it.

---

51. **Which day is the day of rest among Christians?**
Sunday, the first day of the week, on which Christ arose from the dead.

> **Luke 24:1-2**
> **Acts 20:7**
> **I Corinthians 16:2**

52. **How should we keep the day of rest holy?**
1. We must rest from our daily labor, that the time may be used for our instruction in the fear of the Lord.

> **Exodus 23:12a** "Six days you are to do your work, but on the seventh day you shall cease *from labor*."

2. We must earnestly hear and study the Word of God, both in our homes and in church.

> **Luke 11:28b** "Blessed are those who hear the word of God and observe it."

53. **Has the Lord appointed these resting-days to be used only in reading and studying the Word of God?**
No; He has appointed such days also for the needed rest of mind and body.

> **Mark 2:27** Jesus said to them, "The Sabbath was made for man, and not man for the Sabbath."

54. **How do we misuse the day of rest?**
    1. When we neglect and despise the Word of God.

> **Hebrews 10:25** Not forsaking our own assembling together, as is the habit of some, but encouraging *one another;* and all the more as you see the day drawing near.

    2. When we do work or take part in activities that either are actually sinful or turn our minds away from God.

> **Isaiah 56:2b** "[He] keeps from profaning the sabbath, and keeps his hand from doing any evil."

55. **Is any work permitted on Sunday?**
Yes; any work of necessity that cannot be delayed and any loving kindness we may show our neighbor who is in need. Luke 14:1-6

> **James 1:27** Pure and undefiled religion in the sight of *our* God and Father is this: to visit orphans and widows in their distress, *and* to keep oneself unstained by the world.

The Second Table of the Law

56. What is the substance of the second table?
Love to ourselves and our neighbor.

> **Matthew 22:39** "'You shall love your neighbor as yourself.'"

57. May we love ourselves?
Yes; for God has made us, but we must beware of selfishness.

58. What should a man care for most of all?
For his soul, the immortal part of himself.

> **Matthew 16:26a** "For what will it profit a man if he gains the whole world and forfeits his soul?"

59. What does the second table teach us about our relation to our neighbor?
We must feel and act toward him, as we would have him feel and act toward us.

> **Matthew 7:12a** "In everything, therefore, treat people the same way you want them to treat you."
> **I John 3:18** Little children, let us not love with word or with tongue, but in deed and truth.
> **Philippians 2:3-4** Do nothing from selfishness or empty conceit, but with humility of mind regard one another as more important than yourselves; do not *merely* look out for your own personal interests, but also for the interests of others.

60. Who is our neighbor?
Every human being is our neighbor. Read Luke 10:29-37.

61. Must we also love our enemies?
Yes; for even our enemy is our neighbor.

> **Matthew 5:44-45a** "Love your enemies and pray for those who persecute you, so that you may be sons of your Father who is in heaven."

THE FOURTH COMMANDMENT

Honor thy father and thy mother, that thy days may be long upon the land which the LORD thy God giveth thee.

What does this mean?

We should fear and love God so that we do not despise our parents and superiors, nor provoke them to anger, but honor, serve, obey, love, and respect them.

---

62. **Why must we honor father and mother?**
    Because God has placed them over us to care for us.

    > **Leviticus 19:3a** "'Every one of you shall reverence his mother and his father.'"

63. **How are children to show that they honor father and mother?**
    By respectful, loving, and willing obedience and by good behavior to their parents, both in their presence and in their absence.

    > **Proverbs 1:8** Hear, my son, your father's instruction and do not forsake your mother's teaching.
    > **Ephesians 6:1** Children, obey your parents in the Lord, for this is right.

64. **Whom must we honor and obey besides our parents?**
    All those whom God has placed over us, such as guardians, employers, teachers, and the government.

    > **Romans 13:1** Every person is to be in subjection to the governing

authorities. For there is no authority except from God, and those which exist are established by God.

65. Must we obey parents and superiors when they ask us to do what is sinful?
No; we ought to obey God rather than men. Acts 5:29

66. What is the duty of parents toward their children?
They must love them, pray for them, bring them up in the fear of the Lord, and in everything seek their temporal and spiritual good.

> **Proverbs 13:24** He who withholds his rod hates his son, but he who loves him disciplines him diligently.
> **Ephesians 6:4** Fathers, do not provoke your children to anger, but bring them up in the discipline and instruction of the Lord.
> **Deuteronomy 6:6-7** "These words, which I am commanding you today, shall be on your heart. You shall teach them diligently to your sons and shall talk of them when you sit in your house and when you walk by the way and when you lie down and when you rise up."

67. What is God's promise to those who honor father and mother?
It shall be well with them, and they shall live long on the earth.

> **Ephesians 6:1-3** Children, obey your parents in the Lord, for this is right. HONOR YOUR FATHER AND MOTHER (which is the first commandment with a promise), SO THAT IT MAY BE WELL WITH YOU, AND THAT YOU MAY LIVE LONG ON THE EARTH.

68. Is this promise still effective?
Yes; in this sense, that special blessings rest upon obedient children and upon every nation honoring father and mother.

69. Has God also given us a land?
Yes; He has given us our native land, that we may love it and help it to prosper.

70. **What does the fourth commandment forbid?**
    To despise and give offense to father and mother.

    > **Proverbs 17:25** A foolish son is a grief to his father and bitterness to
    > her who bore him.

71. **What does one who transgresses this commandment bring
    upon himself?**
    Condemnation and punishment from God.

    > **Deuteronomy 27:16a** "'Cursed is he who dishonors his father or
    > mother.'"

THE FIFTH COMMANDMENT

Thou shalt not kill.

What does this mean?

We should fear and love God so that we do our neighbor
no bodily harm nor cause him any suffering, but help and
befriend him in every need.

---

72. **How is this commandment transgressed?**
    1. By taking our neighbor's life or by doing him any bodily
       harm.

       > **Genesis 9:6** "Whoever sheds man's blood, by man his blood shall be
       > shed, for in the image of God He made man."

    2. By hatred, anger, abusive words, and all offensive
       behavior toward our neighbor.

       > **I John 3:15** Everyone who hates his brother is a murderer; and you

know that no murderer has eternal life abiding in him.

Ephesians 4:31 Let all bitterness and wrath and anger and clamor and slander be put away from you, along with all malice.

73. **Can we also kill our neighbor's soul?**
Yes; when we cause him to sin, either by purposely leading him astray or by bad example, thus helping to destroy his soul.

> **Romans 16:18b** By their smooth and flattering speech they deceive the hearts of the unsuspecting.
> **Matthew 18:7c** "Woe to that man through whom the stumbling block comes!"

74. **May we take our own life?**
No; God has given us life, and He alone has the right to take it.

> **I Corinthians 6:19-20** Or do you not know that your body is a temple of the Holy Spirit who is in you, whom you have from God, and that you are not your own? For you have been bought with a price: therefore glorify God in your body.

75. **What does God require of us in the fifth commandment?**
That we help our neighbor in time of need and associate with him in love and gentleness.

> **Luke 10:33-37**
> **Ephesians 4:32** Be kind to one another, tender-hearted, forgiving each other, just as God in Christ also has forgiven you.
> **Matthew 25:35-36** "'For I was hungry, and you gave Me *something* to eat; I was thirsty, and you gave Me *something* to drink; I was a stranger, and you invited Me in; naked, and you clothed Me; I was sick, and you visited Me; I was in prison, and you came to Me.'"

THE SIXTH COMMANDMENT

Thou shalt not commit adultery.

What does this mean?

We should fear and love God so that we lead a chaste and pure life in word and deed, and that husband and wife love and honor each other.

---

76. **How is this commandment transgressed?**
    1. When husband and wife are unfaithful to each other.

       Hebrews 13:4 Marriage *is to be held* in honor among all, and the *marriage* bed *is to be* undefiled; for fornicators and adulterers God will judge.

    2. By all impure thoughts, desires, words, and acts, in married as well as in unmarried persons.

       Ephesians 5:3 But immorality or any impurity or greed must not even be named among you, as is proper among saints.

77. **Who has instituted marriage?**
    God Himself instituted it in Paradise. (Garden of Eden)

    Genesis 1:27-28, 2:21-24
    Matthew 19:4-6 "Have you not read that He who created *them* from the beginning MADE THEM MALE AND FEMALE, and said, 'FOR THIS REASON A MAN SHALL LEAVE HIS FATHER AND MOTHER AND BE JOINED TO HIS WIFE, AND THE TWO SHALL BECOME ONE FLESH'? So they are no longer two, but one flesh. What therefore God has joined together, let no man separate."

78. How do unfaithful husbands and wives treat this holy institution?
They despise it and thus bring down upon themselves the judgment of God.

> **Hebrews 13:4b** Fornicators and adulterers God will judge.

79. Repeat some passages from Scripture in which impurity is forbidden.
Do not be deceived: Neither the sexually immoral nor idolaters nor adulterers nor male prostitutes nor homosexual offenders nor thieves nor the greedy nor drunkards nor slanderers nor swindlers will inherit the kingdom of God. I Corinthians 6:9b-10 (NIV)

"But I say to you that everyone who looks at a woman with lust for her has already committed adultery with her in his heart." Matthew 5:28

Let no unwholesome word proceed from your mouth, but only such *a word* as is good for edification according to the need *of the moment*, so that it will give grace to those who hear. Ephesians 4:29

80. Why is this sin so fearful?
Because it affects both soul and body more than any other sin.

> **I Corinthians 6:13-20**

81. How can we be kept pure?
We must watch and pray and avoid everything that awakens impure desires.

> **Matthew 26:41** "Keep watching and praying that you may not enter into temptation; the spirit is willing, but the flesh is weak."
> **Romans 13:14** But put on the Lord Jesus Christ, and make no provision for the flesh in regard to *its* lusts.

82. **What things awaken impure desires?**
Gluttony and drunkenness, immoral amusements, bad
company, the reading of improper books, and everything that
awakens carnal and impure thoughts.

83. **Are not gluttony and drunkenness alone dangerous sins?**
Yes, indeed; they are a shameful abuse of God's gifts by
which we ruin soul and body and shut ourselves out from the
kingdom of God.

> **Luke 21:34** "Be on guard, so that your hearts will not be weighted
> down with dissipation and drunkenness and the worries of life, and that
> day will not come on you suddenly like a trap."

84. **What does God require of us in the sixth commandment?**
We must live a chaste and pure life, whether we are married
or not, with husband and wife loving and honoring each
other.

> **Ephesians 5:33** Nevertheless, each individual among you also is to
> love his own wife even as himself, and the wife must *see to it* that she
> respects her husband.
> **Philippians 4:8** Finally, brethren, whatever is true, whatever is
> honorable, whatever is right, whatever is pure, whatever is lovely,
> whatever is of good repute, if there is any excellence and if anything
> worthy of praise, dwell on these things.

THE SEVENTH COMMANDMENT

Thou shalt not steal.

What does this mean?

We should fear and love God so that we do not rob our neighbor of his money or property, nor bring them into our possession by unfair dealing or fraud, but help him to improve and protect his property and living.

85. **What is it to steal?**
    To steal is to take from our neighbor even the smallest part of his property against his will.

86. **How is stealing done?**
    In a coarse and open or in a deceitful manner.

87. **Who steal in a coarse and open manner?**
    Those who, without any right or permission whatever, take their neighbor's money or property.

    Ephesians 4:28a He who steals must steal no longer.

88. **Who steal in a deceitful manner?**
    Those who take or withhold the property of others by any kind of fraud.

    Proverbs 21:6 The acquisition of treasures by a lying tongue is a fleeting vapor, the pursuit of death.

89. **Is it wrong to be a partner with a thief?**
Yes; the partner of a thief is no better than the thief.

> **Proverbs 29:24a** He who is a partner with a thief hates his own life.

90. **What judgment does the Word of God pass upon the thieves and robbers?**
They shall not inherit the kingdom of God.

> **I Corinthians 6:10** Nor thieves, nor *the* covetous, nor drunkards, nor revilers, nor swindlers, will inherit the kingdom of God.

91. **May we do with our property what we please?**
No; we are but keepers of God's gifts, and we must give an account of how we have used them.

> **Luke 16:2** "And he called him and said to him, 'What is this I hear about you? Give an accounting of your management, for you can no longer be manager.'"
> **Matthew 25:14-30**

92. **What does God require of us in the seventh commandment?**
We must be honest and unselfish in all our dealings and help our neighbor to improve and protect his property and living.

> **I John 3:17** But whoever has the world's goods, and sees his brother in need and closes his heart against him, how does the love of God abide in him?
> **Ephesians 4:28** He who steals must steal no longer; but rather he must labor, performing with his own hands what is good, so that he will have *something* to share with one who has need.

The Eighth Commandment

Thou shalt not bear false witness against thy
neighbor.

What does this mean?

We should fear and love God so that we do not deceitfully
lie about, betray, backbite, nor slander our neighbor but
defend him, speak well of him, and put the most charitable
construction on all that he does.

93. **What is "false witness"?**
    All untruthful speaking about our neighbor, in or out of court.

94. **How does one bear false witness in court?**
    When a witness swears to a lie and when a judge decides
    wrong to be right and right to be wrong.

95. **How do we bear false witness out of court?**
    When we tell lies about our neighbor and slander or defame
    him in our conversation.

    > **Ephesians 4:25** Therefore, laying aside falsehood, SPEAK TRUTH EACH
    > ONE *of you* WITH HIS NEIGHBOR, for we are members of one another.

96. **Do we sin when we speak truthfully of our neighbor's
    faults?**
    Yes; if we do so from an unloving heart, either to injure our
    neighbor or in thoughtlessness and gossip.

Matthew 12:36 "But I tell you that every careless word that people speak, they shall give an accounting for it in the day of judgment."

97. What does God require of us in the eighth commandment?
We must always be truthful, defend and speak well of our neighbor as far as truth permits, and look upon all his acts as well-meant.

> **I Corinthians 13:5-7** [Love] does not act unbecomingly; it does not seek its own, is not provoked, does not take into account a wrong *suffered*, does not rejoice in unrighteousness, but rejoices with the truth; bears all things, believes all things, hopes all things, endures all things.
> **Psalm 51:6** Behold, You desire truth in the innermost being, and in the hidden part You will make me know wisdom.

THE NINTH COMMANDMENT

Thou shalt not covet thy neighbor's house.

What does this mean?

We should fear and love God so that we do not seek by craftiness to gain possession of our neighbor's inheritance or home, nor obtain them under pretense of a legal right, but assist and serve him in keeping the same.

The Tenth Commandment

Thou shalt not covet thy neighbor's wife, nor his manservant, nor his maidservant, nor his cattle, nor anything that is thy neighbor's.

What does this mean?

We should fear and love God so that we do not estrange or entice away our neighbor's wife, servants, or cattle, but seek to have them remain and fulfill their duty to him.

98. **What do the ninth and tenth commandments forbid?**
    All sinful desire to get what belongs to our neighbor.

    I Kings 21:1-14

99. **What does God require of us in the ninth and tenth commandments?**
    We must heartily wish our neighbor all good, rejoice in his success, and help him to keep what he owns.

    I Corinthians 10:24 Let no one seek his own *good*, but that of his neighbor.
    Romans 12:15 Rejoice with those who rejoice, and weep with those who weep.

100. **What, then, does God require of us in His holy Law?**
    Perfect purity and holiness in all our thoughts and desires, words and acts.

    James 2:10 For whoever keeps the whole law and yet stumbles in one *point*, he has become guilty of all.

Matthew 5:48 "Therefore you are to be perfect, as your heavenly Father is perfect."

THE CONCLUSION

101. What does God say of all these Commandments?

I the LORD thy God am a jealous God, visiting the iniquity of the fathers upon the children unto the third and fourth generation of them that hate Me; and showing mercy unto thousands of them that love Me and keep My commandments.

What does this mean?

God threatens to punish all who transgress these commandments. We should, therefore, fear His wrath, and in no way disobey them. But He promises grace and every blessing to all who keep them. We should, therefore, love Him, trust in Him, and gladly keep His commandments.

---

102. Of what does God remind us by these words?

He reminds us of the fact that He is a just God, who in His holy wrath punishes every sin.

Joshua 24:19-20

103. What is sin?
Sin is any thought or feeling, word or act, which is contrary to God's holy Law.

> **I John 5:17a** All unrighteousness is sin.

104. What is meant by original sin?
Original sin is the inborn wickedness, deep corruption, and evil disposition of the human heart.

> **Psalm 51:5** Behold, I was brought forth in iniquity, and in sin my mother conceived me.
> **Romans 5:12** Therefore, just as through one man sin entered into the world, and death through sin, and so death spread to all men, because all sinned.

105. What is actual sin?
Actual sin is all evil thoughts and desires, words and acts, springing from original sin.

> **I John 3:4** Everyone who practices sin also practices lawlessness; and sin is lawlessness.

106. Is neglecting to do good as sinful as doing wrong?
Yes, indeed; to the one who knows to do good and does not do it, to him it is sin. James 4:17

107. Do the children of God always live according to the will of their heavenly Father?
They hate sin and heartily strive to keep the Law of God; but it is their experience that they sin every day and that the new life within them is weak.

> **Psalm 19:12** Who can discern *his* errors? Acquit me of hidden *faults.*
> **Romans 7:19** For the good that I want, I do not do, but I practice the very evil that I do not want.

108. **How do the children of God feel and act when they find that they have sinned?**

They are deeply grieved, they ask their heavenly Father to forgive them, and they earnestly strive to put off sin.

> **I John 1:9** If we confess our sins, He is faithful and righteous to forgive us our sins and to cleanse us from all unrighteousness.
> **Romans 6:12** Therefore do not let sin reign in your mortal body so that you obey its lusts.
> **Romans 6:1-2**
> **Romans 7:18-25**

109. **What do the children of the world think of sin?**

They love sin and do not ask to be forgiven.

> **Proverbs 14:9a** Fools mock at sin.

110. **How does God threaten those who transgress His commandments?**

He will visit, that is, punish their wickedness.

> **Ephesians 5:5-6** For this you know with certainty, that no immoral or impure person or covetous man, who is an idolater, has an inheritance in the kingdom of Christ and God. Let no one deceive you with empty words, for because of these things the wrath of God comes upon the sons of disobedience.

111. **How does God punish sin?**

In soul and body, now and forever.

> **Galatians 3:10b** "Cursed is everyone who does not abide by all things written in the book of the law, to perform them."
> **Ezekiel 18:20a** "The person who sins will die."

112. **What does God promise all who keep His commandments?**

He will have mercy upon them to a thousand generations.
Deuteronomy 7:9

113. **What is here understood by mercy?**
Every blessing for soul and body, now and forever.

> **Ephesians 2:4-5** But God, being rich in mercy, because of His great
> love with which He loved us, even when we were dead in our
> transgressions, made us alive together with Christ (by grace you have
> been saved).

114. **What way of salvation does the Law then point out to us?**
Keep the commandments and you shall be saved.

> **Luke 10:28b** "Do this and you will live."

115. **Can anyone, then, keep God's commandments so
perfectly that he is thereby justified and saved?**
No; everyone is a sinner and lacks that perfect love which is
the fulfillment of the law.

> **Romans 10:3** For not knowing about God's righteousness and seeking
> to establish their own, they did not subject themselves to the
> righteousness of God.
> **James 2:10** For whoever keeps the whole law and yet stumbles in one
> *point*, he has become guilty of all.

116. **But does the Word of God point out a way to us in which
a sinner may be justified and saved?**
Yes; in the blessed Gospel.

> **Romans 1:16a** For I am not ashamed of the gospel, for it is the power
> of God for salvation to everyone who believes.
> **II Corinthians 5:21** He made Him who knew no sin *to be* sin on our
> behalf, so that we might become the righteousness of God in Him.
> **Philippians 3:9** [That I] may be found in Him, not having a
> righteousness of my own derived from *the* Law, but that which is
> through faith in Christ, the righteousness which *comes* from God on the
> basis of faith.

117. **What parts of the catechism teach about the Gospel?**
The last four parts: the Apostles' Creed, the Lord's Prayer,
Baptism, and the Lord's Supper.

Part Two

THE THREE ARTICLES
OF THE APOSTLES' CREED

118. What do the three articles teach?
The nature, will, and works of the Triune God.

119. How do you know there is a God?
1. From the world's creation, its preservation and order.

    Romans 1:19-20 Because that which is known about God is evident within them; for God made it evident to them. For since the creation of the world His invisible attributes, His eternal power and divine nature, have been clearly seen, being understood through what has been made, so that they are without excuse.

2. From my conscience, which is troubled when I do evil and rejoices when I do good.

    Romans 2:15 In that they show the work of the Law written in their hearts, their conscience bearing witness and their thoughts alternately accusing or else defending them.

3. From the holy Scriptures wherein He still more clearly reveals Himself.

    John 1:18 No one has seen God at any time; the only begotten God who is in the bosom of the Father, He has explained *Him.*

120. What is God?
God is a spirit, who is eternal and almighty; all-knowing and everywhere present; wise, good, and merciful; holy, true, and just.

John 4:24 "God is spirit, and those who worship Him must worship in spirit and truth."

Psalm 90:2 Before the mountains were born or You gave birth to the earth and the world, even from everlasting to everlasting, You are God.

Luke 1:37 "For nothing will be impossible with God."

I John 3:20b For God is greater than our heart and knows all things.

Psalm 139:7 Where can I go from Your Spirit? Or where can I flee from Your presence?

Psalm 104:24a O LORD, how many are Your works! In wisdom You have made them all.

I John 4:16b God is love.

Psalm 106:1 Praise the LORD! Oh give thanks to the LORD, for He is good; for His lovingkindness is everlasting.

Psalm 103:13 Just as a father has compassion on *his* children, so the LORD has compassion on those who fear Him.

Isaiah 6:3b "Holy, Holy, Holy, is the LORD of hosts, the whole earth is full of His glory."

Numbers 23:19 "God is not a man, that He should lie, nor a son of man, that He should repent; has He said, and will He not do it? Or has He spoken, and will He not make it good?"

Romans 2:6 [God] WILL RENDER TO EACH PERSON ACCORDING TO HIS DEEDS.

121. Are there more Gods than one?

No; there is only one God, and there is none other besides Him.

Deuteronomy 6:4 "Hear, O Israel! The LORD is our God, the LORD is one!"

122. How many persons are there in the Godhead?

Three: the Father, the Son, and the Holy Spirit. These three are perfectly alike in character and equal in greatness.

Matthew 28:19 "Go therefore and make disciples of all the nations, baptizing them in the name of the Father and the Son and the Holy Spirit."

II Corinthians 13:14 The grace of the Lord Jesus Christ, and the love of God, and the fellowship of the Holy Spirit, be with you all.

THE FIRST ARTICLE OF CREATION

I believe in God the Father Almighty, Maker of heaven and earth.

What does this mean?

I believe that God has created me and all that exists; that He has given and still preserves to me my body and soul, my eyes and ears, and all my members, my reason and all the powers of my soul, together with food and clothing, home and family, and all my property; that He daily provides abundantly for all the needs of my life, protects me from all danger, and guards and keeps me from all evil; and that He does this purely out of fatherly and divine goodness and mercy, without any merit or worthiness in me; for all of which I am in duty bound to thank, praise, serve, and obey Him. This is most certainly true.

123. **What do you mean when you say, "I believe in God the Father"?**

I believe that God is the Father of Jesus Christ, and my Father; and I surrender myself to Him, trusting with all my heart in His grace and love.

> **Romans 8:15-16** For you have not received a spirit of slavery leading to fear again, but you have received a spirit of adoption as sons by which we cry out, "Abba! Father!" The Spirit Himself testifies with our spirit that we are children of God.

124. Why do we call God the Maker of heaven and earth?
Because He has made heaven and earth to come forth by His almighty word.

> **Psalm 33:9** For He spoke, and it was done; He commanded, and it stood fast.

125. Does God still care for what He made?
Yes; by His watchful care, He preserves and governs all things.

> **Isaiah 40:26** Lift up your eyes on high and see who has created these *stars*, the One who leads forth their host by number, He calls them all by name; because of the greatness of His might and the strength of *His* power, not one *of them* is missing.
> **Colossians 1:17** He is before all things, and in Him all things hold together.

126. How does God preserve all things?
He lets all things continue as long as He thinks best, and He cares like a father for all His creatures.

> **Genesis 8:22** "While the earth remains, seedtime and harvest, and cold and heat, and summer and winter, and day and night shall not cease."
> **Acts 17:25b** He Himself gives to all *people* life and breath and all things.
> **Psalm 104:27** They all wait for You to give them their food in due season.

127. For whom does God care most?
For mankind, and especially for His believing children.

> **Matthew 6:26** "Look at the birds of the air, that they do not sow, nor reap nor gather into barns, and *yet* your heavenly Father feeds them. Are you not worth much more than they?"

128. How does God govern men with regard to their sins?
He allows them to sin, sets limits to their sinning, and so guides the result that everything will be for their good who love Him.

Genesis 50:20a "You meant evil against me, *but* God meant it for good."

Romans 8:28 And we know that God causes all things to work together for good to those who love God, to those who are called according to *His* purpose.

129. Do we always understand God's ways?

No; His ways are often hidden from our eyes, but even then they are the kindest and best.

Isaiah 55:8-9 "For My thoughts are not your thoughts, nor are your ways My ways," declares the LORD. "For *as* the heavens are higher than the earth, so are My ways higher than your ways and My thoughts than your thoughts."

130. In whose care may you therefore safely leave yourself?

In God's care, who protects me from all danger and keeps me from all evil.

I Peter 5:7 Casting all your anxiety on Him, because He cares for you.

Psalm 27:1 The LORD is my light and my salvation; whom shall I fear? The LORD is the defense of my life; whom shall I dread?

131. Have you deserved all this?

Not in the least; He does all this, not because I have deserved it, but because He is a loving and merciful Father.

Genesis 32:10a "I am unworthy of all the lovingkindness and of all the faithfulness which You have shown to Your servant."

132. What do you owe God for all this goodness?

It is my duty to serve Him thankfully and obediently all the days of my life.

Psalm 103:2 Bless the LORD, O my soul, and forget none of His benefits.

Romans 12:1 Therefore I urge you, brethren, by the mercies of God, to present your bodies a living and holy sacrifice, acceptable to God, *which is* your spiritual service of worship.

133. Which are the most excellent of the heavenly creatures?
The holy angels.

134. What is the work of the holy angels?
They praise God and serve Him, especially by ministering to
His children.

> **Psalm 103:20** Bless the LORD, you His angels, mighty in strength, who
> perform His word, obeying the voice of His word!
> **Matthew 18:10** "See that you do not despise one of these little ones,
> for I say to you that their angels in heaven continually see the face of
> My Father who is in heaven."
> **Hebrews 1:14** Are they not all ministering spirits, sent out to render
> service for the sake of those who will inherit salvation?

135. Are there also evil angels?
Yes; there are evil angels who have fallen away from God
through pride and disobedience. They are forever excluded
from fellowship with Him. The devil is their king.

> **Matthew 25:41** "Then He will also say to those on His left, 'Depart
> from Me, accursed ones, into the eternal fire which has been prepared
> for the devil and his angels.'"
> **II Corinthians 11:14** No wonder, for even Satan disguises himself as
> an angel of light.
> **II Peter 2:4** For if God did not spare angels when they sinned, but cast
> them into hell and committed them to pits of darkness, reserved for
> judgment.

136. Which is the most excellent of the earthly creatures?
Man, to whom God gave power to rule over the earth.

> **Psalm 8:4-6** What is man that You take thought of him, and the son of
> man that You care for him? Yet You have made him a little lower than
> God, and You crown him with glory and majesty! You make him to rule
> over the works of Your hands; You have put all things under his feet.

137. What was the character of man as he was made by God?
Adam and Eve were innocent, without sin, and like God.

> **Genesis 1:27** God created man in His own image, in the image of God He created him; male and female He created them.

138. In what did the image of God in man consist?

In true wisdom, righteousness and holiness, peace and joy.

> **Ephesians 4:24** And put on the new self, which in *the likeness of* God has been created in righteousness and holiness of the truth.

139. What benefit did the human body have from the image of God?

Perfect health, immortality, and a life free from care in Paradise. (Garden of Eden)

140. Did our first parents remain innocent and without sin?

No; they sinned and lost the image of God, and thus sin and death entered into the world.

> **Genesis 2:17b** "For in the day that you eat from it you will surely die."
> **Romans 6:23a** For the wages of sin is death.
> **Romans 5:12** Therefore, just as through one man sin entered into the world, and death through sin, and so death spread to all men, because all sinned.

141. In what did their sin consist?

It consisted especially in the unbelief of their hearts and in their selfishness and disobedience.

142. Who led them astray?

They permitted the devil to lead them astray.

> **Genesis 3:1-5**
> **John 8:44b** "[The devil] was a murderer from the beginning, and does not stand in the truth because there is no truth in him. Whenever he speaks a lie, he speaks from his own *nature*, for he is a liar and the father of lies."

143. How has sin injured the human soul?

1. It has darkened the understanding.

   I Corinthians 2:14 But a natural man does not accept the things of the Spirit of God, for they are foolishness to him; and he cannot understand them, because they are spiritually appraised.

2. It has made the will incapable of what is good and desirous of all that is evil.

   Romans 8:7a Because the mind set on the flesh is hostile toward God.

3. It has disturbed the peace and joy of conscience.

   Genesis 3:8, 10 They heard the sound of the LORD God walking in the garden in the cool of the day, and the man and his wife hid themselves from the presence of the LORD God among the trees of the garden. [Adam] said, "I heard the sound of You in the garden, and I was afraid because I was naked; so I hid myself."

144. How has sin injured the human body?

Sin has made the body a tool of every evil desire and has brought upon it disease, distress, countless pains, and finally death.

Job 14:1-2 "Man, who is born of woman, is short-lived and full of turmoil. Like a flower he comes forth and withers. He also flees like a shadow and does not remain."

145. Have all men become sinners through the fall of our first parents?

Yes; sin and death have spread from our first parents to the whole human race.

Romans 5:18a So then as through one transgression there resulted condemnation to all men.
Romans 5:12 Therefore, just as through one man sin entered into the world, and death through sin, and so death spread to all men, because all sinned.

146. Will God, then, leave all men to perish?

No; God has in love sent His Son Jesus Christ to save man.

> **John 3:16** "For God so loved the world, that He gave His only begotten Son, that whoever believes in Him shall not perish, but have eternal life."

147. When was the Savior first promised to the world?

Immediately after the Fall.

> **Genesis 3:15 (NKJV)** "And I will put enmity between you and the woman, and between your seed and her Seed; He shall bruise your head, and you shall bruise His heel."

148. When was Christ sent to the world?

In the fullness of time; that is, the time appointed and prepared by God Himself.

> **Galatians 4:4a** But when the fullness of the time came, God sent forth His Son, born of a woman.

The Second Article of Redemption

And in Jesus Christ His only Son, our Lord; Who was conceived by the Holy Spirit, Born of the Virgin Mary; Suffered under Pontius Pilate, Was crucified, dead, and buried; He descended into hell; The third day He rose again from the dead; He ascended into heaven, And is seated on the right hand of God the Father Almighty; From where He shall come to judge the living and the dead.

What does this mean?

I believe that Jesus Christ, true God, begotten of the Father from eternity, and also true Man, born of the Virgin Mary, is my Lord; who has redeemed me, a lost and condemned creature, bought me and freed me from all sins, from death, and from the power of the devil; not with silver and gold, but with His holy and precious blood and with His innocent sufferings and death; in order that I might be His own, live under Him in His kingdom, and serve Him in everlasting righteousness, innocence, and blessedness; even as He is risen from the dead and lives and reigns to all eternity. This is most certainly true.

149. **What do you mean when you say, "I believe in Jesus Christ"?**
     Trusting in Jesus Christ with all my heart, I surrender myself to Him as my only Savior from sin, and death, and the power of Satan.

Acts 4:12 "And there is salvation in no one else; for there is no other name under heaven that has been given among men by which we must be saved."

Romans 10:9 That if you confess with your mouth Jesus *as* Lord, and believe in your heart that God raised Him from the dead, you will be saved.

150. Who is Jesus Christ?

The Son of God and the Son of Mary, true God and true man.

> **Matthew 1:20-23**

151. How does Christ have divine nature?

He is begotten of the Father from eternity.

> **John 1:1** In the beginning was the Word, and the Word was with God, and the Word was God.
> **Colossians 2:9** For in Him all the fullness of Deity dwells in bodily form.

152. How does Christ have human nature?

He is conceived by the Holy Spirit and born of the Virgin Mary.

> **Galatians 4:4a** But when the fullness of the time came, God sent forth His Son, born of a woman.
> **Matthew 1:20** But when he had considered this, behold, an angel of the Lord appeared to him in a dream, saying, "Joseph, son of David, do not be afraid to take Mary as your wife; for the Child who has been conceived in her is of the Holy Spirit."

153. What does the Bible say about Christ being true God?

The Bible calls Him the only begotten Son of God and one with the Father.

The Bible also expressly calls Him "God."

> **John 10:30** "I and the Father are one."
> **John 5:23** "So that all will honor the Son even as they honor the Father. He who does not honor the Son does not honor the Father who sent Him."
> **I John 5:20b** This is the true God and eternal life.

John 1:1 In the beginning was the Word, and the Word was with God, and the Word was God.
John 3:16

154. What does the Bible say about Christ being both God and man?

It says, "And the Word became flesh, and dwelt among us" (John 1:14a) and "But when the fullness of the time came, God sent forth His son, born of a woman" (Galatians 4:4a).

155. Why did the Son of God become true man?

In order that He might suffer and die for us.

Romans 5:6-8 For while we were still helpless, at the right time Christ died for the ungodly. For one will hardly die for a righteous man; though perhaps for the good man someone would dare even to die. But God demonstrates His own love toward us, in that while we were yet sinners, Christ died for us.
Hebrews 2:14-17

156. Why must our Savior also be true God?

In order that His death and His blood might have everlasting power to atone for sin.

Romans 5:17 For if by the transgression of the one, death reigned through the one, much more those who receive the abundance of grace and of the gift of righteousness will reign in life through the One, Jesus Christ.
Hebrews 9:12 And not through the blood of goats and calves, but through His own blood, He entered the holy place once for all, having obtained eternal redemption.
II Corinthians 5:21 He made Him who knew no sin *to be* sin on our behalf, so that we might become the righteousness of God in Him.

157. Was Jesus conceived and born with sin?

No; He was conceived by the Holy Spirit and therefore without sin.

> **Luke 1:35** The angel answered and said to [Mary], "The Holy Spirit will come upon you, and the power of the Most High will overshadow you; and for that reason the holy Child shall be called the Son of God."

158. What does the name "Jesus" signify?

A Savior.

> **Matthew 1:21** "She will bear a Son; and you shall call His name Jesus, for He will save His people from their sins."

159. What does the name "Christ" signify?

The same as Messiah; that is, the Anointed or the Consecrated.

160. How was Jesus anointed?

He was anointed with the Holy Spirit and with power. Acts 10:38

161. For what offices was Jesus anointed and consecrated?

The offices of High Priest, Prophet, and King.

162. What is Christ's work as High Priest?

He offered up Himself as a sacrifice for our sins, and He always prays for us.

> **Hebrews 7:26-27** For it was fitting for us to have such a high priest, holy, innocent, undefiled, separated from sinners and exalted above the heavens; who does not need daily, like those high priests, to offer up sacrifices, first for His own sins and then for the *sins* of the people, because this He did once for all when He offered up Himself.
> **Romans 8:34** Christ Jesus is He who died, yes, rather who was raised, who is at the right hand of God, who also intercedes for us.

163. What is Christ's work as Prophet?

He teaches us the will of God concerning our salvation.

> **Luke 24:19b** "Jesus the Nazarene, who was a prophet mighty in deed and word in the sight of God and all the people."

164. What is Christ's work as King?
He governs and keeps His children and defends them against their enemies.

> **Luke 1:33** "And He will reign over the house of Jacob forever, and His kingdom will have no end."
> **Revelation 17:14b** "He is Lord of lords and King of kings."

165. What name is given to believers in Christ?
They are called Christians, meaning "the anointed ones."

> **I John 2:20 (NIV)** But you have an anointing from the Holy One, and all of you know the truth.
> **Acts 11:26c** And the disciples were first called Christians in Antioch.

166. With what means has Christ redeemed us?
He has paid for our sins with His holy and precious blood and His innocent death, and He has fulfilled the Law in our place with His holy life and His perfect obedience.

> **I Peter 1:18-19** Knowing that you were not redeemed with perishable things like silver or gold from your futile way of life inherited from your forefathers, but with precious blood, as of a lamb unblemished and spotless, *the blood* of Christ.

167. Whom has Christ redeemed?
He has redeemed me, a lost and condemned sinner.

> **Isaiah 43:1** But now, thus says the LORD, your Creator, O Jacob, and He who formed you, O Israel, "Do not fear, for I have redeemed you; I have called you by name; you are Mine!"
> **I Timothy 1:15** It is a trustworthy statement, deserving full acceptance, that Christ Jesus came into the world to save sinners, among whom I am foremost *of all.*

168. Has not Christ redeemed all mankind?
Yes, He has; He gave Himself a ransom for all. I Timothy 2:6

> **I John 2:2** And He Himself is the propitiation for our sins; and not for ours only, but also for *those of* the whole world.

169. But are not many, thus redeemed, yet lost?
Yes, indeed; many reject Him because of their unbelief and love of sin.

> **II Peter 2:1b** Even denying the Master who bought them, bringing swift destruction upon themselves.
> **John 3:18** "He who believes in Him is not judged; he who does not believe has been judged already, because he has not believed in the name of the only begotten Son of God."

170. Who share in the redemption of Christ?
Those who repent of their sins and believe in Him.

> **Mark 1:15b** "Repent and believe in the gospel."
> **John 6:37** "All that the Father gives Me will come to Me, and the one who comes to Me I will certainly not cast out."
> **Ephesians 1:7** In Him we have redemption through His blood, the forgiveness of our trespasses, according to the riches of His grace.

171. What benefits does the believer have from the redemption of Christ?
By this redemption he is freed from sin, from death, and from the power of Satan.

172. In what way is the believer freed from sin by the redemption of Christ?
1. The guilt and punishment of sin are removed from him.

> **Colossians 1:14** In whom we have redemption, the forgiveness of sins.

2. Sin rules over him no longer.

> **Romans 6:14a** For sin shall not be master over you.

3. When he dies, sin is entirely rooted out from him.

> **I John 3:2** Beloved, now we are children of God, and it has not appeared as yet what we will be. We know that when He appears, we will be like Him, because we will see Him just as He is.
> **I Corinthians 15:42-57**

173. In what way is the believer freed from death by the redemption of Christ?

Spiritual death has lost its power over him, temporal death is but an entrance into perfect life, and eternal death he no longer fears.

> **John 11:25-26** Jesus said to her, "I am the resurrection and the life; he who believes in Me will live even if he dies, and everyone who lives and believes in Me will never die. Do you believe this?"

174. In what way is the believer freed from the power of Satan by the redemption of Christ?

Satan has no power over the believer, unless the believer yields himself into his service.

> **Hebrews 2:14** Therefore, since the children share in flesh and blood, He Himself likewise also partook of the same, that through death He might render powerless him who had the power of death, that is, the devil.

175. For what purpose has Christ redeemed you?

He has redeemed me in order that I might be His own, live under Him in His kingdom, and serve Him in everlasting righteousness, innocence, and blessedness.

> **I Corinthians 6:20** For you have been bought with a price: therefore glorify God in your body.
> **Titus 2:14** Who gave Himself for us to redeem us from every lawless deed, and to purify for Himself a people for His own possession, zealous for good deeds.

176. What did Christ do in order to become our Savior and Redeemer?

He humbled Himself by becoming obedient to the point of death, even death on a cross. Philippians 2:8

177. How many steps do you notice in the humiliation of Christ?

Five: His birth in poverty, His suffering, His crucifixion, His death, and His burial.

178. Why did Christ begin His life on earth with the birth in poverty?

He began His life in poverty to show that His kingdom is not of this world, and that we might be made rich through His poverty.

> **II Corinthians 8:9** For you know the grace of our Lord Jesus Christ, that though He was rich, yet for your sake He became poor, so that you through His poverty might become rich.

179. When was the suffering of Christ greatest?

In the night before His death and on Good Friday, when He was delivered into the hands of His enemies, and was bound, beaten, scourged, crowned with thorns, and finally nailed to the cross.

> **Matthew 27:1-46**

180. Did Christ suffer bodily pain only?

No; His greatest suffering was a fearful anguish of soul on account of our sins.

> **Matthew 27:46** About the ninth hour Jesus cried out with a loud voice, saying, "ELI, ELI, LAMA SABACHTHANI?" that is, "MY GOD, MY GOD, WHY HAVE YOU FORSAKEN ME?"
> **II Corinthians 5:21** He made Him who knew no sin *to be* sin on our behalf, so that we might become the righteousness of God in Him.

181. When in particular did He suffer this anguish?

In the garden, when His sweat became as drops of blood and He said, "My soul is deeply grieved to the point of death" (Mark 14:34), and on the cross, when He cried, "MY GOD,

My God, why have You forsaken Me?" (Mark 15:34).

> **Isaiah 53:4-5** Surely our griefs He Himself bore, and our sorrows He carried; yet we ourselves esteemed Him stricken, smitten of God, and afflicted. But He was pierced through for our transgressions, He was crushed for our iniquities; the chastening for our well-being *fell* upon Him, and by His scourging we are healed.

182. How did Christ act through all this suffering?

He was patient as a lamb that is led to the slaughter.

> **Isaiah 53:7** He was oppressed and He was afflicted, yet He did not open His mouth; like a lamb that is led to slaughter, and like a sheep that is silent before its shearers, so He did not open His mouth.

183. What did Christ accomplish for us by His death on the cross?

By His death He has paid the wages of sin, which is death.

> **Romans 5:10a** For if while we were enemies we were reconciled to God through the death of His Son.
>
> **I John 2:2** And He Himself is the propitiation for our sins; and not for ours only, but also for *those of* the whole world.

184. What comfort do we have from the burial of Christ?

He has buried our sins, hallowed our graves, and taken away their horror.

> **Romans 6:4** Therefore we have been buried with Him through baptism into death, so that as Christ was raised from the dead through the glory of the Father, so we too might walk in newness of life.

185. How should we look upon the life and suffering of Christ in His humiliation?

We should look upon His life and His suffering as an atonement for our sins and as an example to the believer of holiness in life and patience in suffering.

> **I Peter 2:21b** Christ also suffered for you, leaving you an example for you to follow in His steps.

186. Did Christ remain in humiliation and death?

No; God exalted Him and gave unto Him the name which is above every name. Philippians 2:9

187. How many steps do you notice in the exaltation of Christ?

Five: His descent into hell, His resurrection, His ascension, His reign at the right hand of the Father, and His coming to judge the living and the dead.

188. What did Christ accomplish when He descended into hell?

He made known the victory which He had won over the devil and proclaimed it to the spirits in prison. I Peter 3:18-19

189. What benefit do we have from the resurrection of Christ?

1. The resurrection assures us that Christ is the Son of God, and that He has conquered death and made full satisfaction for our sins.

   Romans 1:4 Who was declared the Son of God with power by the resurrection from the dead, according to the Spirit of holiness, Jesus Christ our Lord.

2. The resurrection gives us power to arise from spiritual death and to live a new and holy life.

   Romans 6:4b As Christ was raised from the dead through the glory of the Father, so we too might walk in newness of life.

3. The resurrection assures us that our bodies shall arise in glory on the last day.

   John 6:40 "For this is the will of My Father, that everyone who beholds the Son and believes in Him will have eternal life, and I Myself will raise him up on the last day."

190. What command did Christ give His disciples before His ascension?

He commanded them to go out into the whole world and preach the Gospel to all nations. (Missions)

> **Matthew 28:19**
> **Mark 16:15**

191. What is meant by the ascension of Christ?

He left the earth, so that He is no longer visibly present, and He entered into His Father's glory to prepare a place for us in the heavenly mansions.

> **John 14:2** "In My Father's house are many dwelling places; if it were not so, I would have told you; for I go to prepare a place for you."

192. What does the ascension of Christ teach us?

It teaches us to be heavenly-minded and to have a desire to depart and be with Christ.

> **Colossians 3:1** Therefore if you have been raised up with Christ, keep seeking the things above, where Christ is, seated at the right hand of God.

193. What is the significance of Christ's reign on the right hand of the Father?

It signifies that He shares also as true man in the power and glory of God and rules over all things.

> **I Peter 3:22** [He] is at the right hand of God, having gone into heaven, after angels and authorities and powers had been subjected to Him.

194. What benefit do we have from Christ's reign on the right hand of the Father?

He protects His kingdom from its enemies, prays for us, and sends us His Holy Spirit.

> **Hebrews 7:25** Therefore He is able also to save forever those who draw near to God through Him, since He always lives to make intercession for them.

195. Is Christ still present on earth?
Yes; He is present in a real, though invisible, manner.

> **Matthew 28:20b** "And lo, I am with you always, even to the end of the age."

196. When will He come to earth again in a visible manner?
On the last day, when He comes to judge the living and the dead.

> **Luke 21:27** "Then they will see THE SON OF MAN COMING IN A CLOUD with power and great glory."
> **II Corinthians 5:10** For we must all appear before the judgment seat of Christ, so that each one may be recompensed for his deeds in the body, according to what he has done, whether good or bad.

197. By what rule will Christ judge us?
He will judge us by His Word.

> **John 12:48b** "The word I spoke is what will judge him at the last day."
> **Revelation 20:12** And I saw the dead, the great and the small, standing before the throne, and books were opened; and another book was opened, which is *the book* of life; and the dead were judged from the things which were written in the books, according to their deeds.

198. Is it enough that you know all these things about Christ and hold them to be true?
No; the Holy Spirit must teach me to know Christ in a true and living faith.

> **Romans 8:9b** But if anyone does not have the Spirit of Christ, he does not belong to Him.
> **Romans 8:14** For all who are being led by the Spirit of God, these are sons of God.

The Third Article of Sanctification

I believe in the Holy Spirit; The holy Christian Church, The Communion of Saints; The Forgiveness of sins; The Resurrection of the body; And the Life everlasting. Amen.

What does this mean?

I believe that I cannot by my own reason or strength believe in Jesus Christ my Lord, or come to Him; but the Holy Spirit has called me through the Gospel, enlightened me with His gifts, and sanctified and preserved me in the true faith; in like manner as He calls, gathers, enlightens, and sanctifies the whole Christian Church on earth, and preserves it in union with Jesus Christ in the one true faith; in this Christian Church, He daily forgives abundantly all my sins and the sins of all believers, and at the last day will raise up me and all the dead and will grant everlasting life to me and to all who believe in Christ. This is most certainly true.

199. **What do you mean when you say, "I believe in the Holy Spirit"?**

I trust with all my heart in the Holy Spirit as my guide and my sanctifier, who gives me strength to believe in Jesus and to live according to His will.

> **I Corinthians 12:3b** And no one can say, "Jesus is Lord," except by the Holy Spirit.

200. Who is the Holy Spirit?

The Holy Spirit is true God together with the Father and the Son.

> **I Corinthians 2:10b** For the Spirit searches all things, even the depths of God.
> **I Corinthians 3:16** Do you not know that you are a temple of God and *that* the Spirit of God dwells in you?
> **John 15:26** "When the Helper comes, whom I will send to you from the Father, *that is* the Spirit of truth who proceeds from the Father, He will testify about Me."

201. What is the work of the Holy Spirit?

To call, enlighten, sanctify, and preserve.

202. How does the Holy Spirit call us?

The Holy Spirit calls us by awakening in our hearts a deep sense of sin and by inviting us to receive the grace of God in Christ.

> **John 16:8-9** "And He, when He comes, will convict the world concerning sin and righteousness and judgment; concerning sin, because they do not believe in Me."
> **Ephesians 5:14b** "Awake, sleeper, and arise from the dead, and Christ will shine on you."

203. By what means does the Holy Spirit call us?

By the Word of God, using the Law to awaken our hearts and the Gospel to invite us to Christ.

> **Romans 3:20b** For through the Law *comes* the knowledge of sin.
> **II Thessalonians 2:14** It was for this He called you through our gospel, that you may gain the glory of our Lord Jesus Christ.
> **Matthew 22:1-14**

204. What means does God use to make us heed the call of the Holy Spirit?

He often uses suffering, often blessings, often the example of others, and other means that may lead us to reflect.

Psalm 119:71 It is good for me that I was afflicted, that I may learn Your statutes.

Romans 2:4 Or do you think lightly of the riches of His kindness and tolerance and patience, not knowing that the kindness of God leads you to repentance?

205. Do all obey the call of the Holy Spirit?

No; many resist the Holy Spirit and will not repent and come to Christ.

Acts 7:51a "You men who are stiff-necked and uncircumcised in heart and ears are always resisting the Holy Spirit."

Isaiah 65:2 "I have spread out My hands all day long to a rebellious people, who walk *in* the way which is not good, following their own thoughts."

Romans 3:10-18

206. When does a person harden his heart?

A person hardens his heart when he persistently despises and opposes the voice of the Holy Spirit in his conscience.

Acts 28:25-27

207. Who obey the call of the Holy Spirit?

They who repent of their sins and believe the Gospel.

Mark 1:15 "The time is fulfilled, and the kingdom of God is at hand; repent and believe in the gospel."

208. What is it to repent?

He who truly repents feels his sins with shame and sorrow, freely confesses his sins to God, and earnestly seeks the grace of God in Christ.

Isaiah 55:7 Let the wicked forsake his way and the unrighteous man his thoughts; and let him return to the LORD, and He will have compassion on him, and to our God, for He will abundantly pardon.

II Corinthians 7:10 For the sorrow that is according to *the will of* God produces a repentance without regret, *leading* to salvation, but the sorrow of the world produces death.

> **Psalm 32:5** I acknowledged my sin to You, and my iniquity I did not hide; I said, "I will confess my transgressions to the LORD"; and You forgave the guilt of my sin.

209. How do we learn that the grace of God is found in Christ?
We learn this through the enlightenment of the Holy Spirit.

> **I Corinthians 2:12** Now we have received, not the spirit of the world, but the Spirit who is from God, so that we may know the things freely given to us by God.

210. What is meant by the enlightenment of the Holy Spirit?
Through the enlightenment of the Holy Spirit, our knowledge of the Gospel truths becomes a living and saving knowledge to our hearts.

> **John 14:26** "But the Helper, the Holy Spirit, whom the Father will send in My name, He will teach you all things, and bring to your remembrance all that I said to you."
> **John 16:13a** "But when He, the Spirit of truth, comes, He will guide you into all the truth."

211. Of what nature is our knowledge of these truths before the Holy Spirit has enlightened our hearts?
It is a dead knowledge only, which does not lead to repentance and faith, but leaves us in our sins.

> **I Corinthians 1:18a** For the word of the cross is foolishness to those who are perishing.

212. What is the true and living faith in Jesus Christ?
This is true and living faith:

That a repentant sinner lays hold of Christ as his only Savior from sin, death, and the power of Satan; and

That he takes refuge in Christ and His righteousness and builds thereon with the confidence of his whole heart.

I John 4:15-16 Whoever confesses that Jesus is the Son of God, God abides in him, and he in God. We have come to know and have believed the love which God has for us. God is love, and the one who abides in love abides in God, and God abides in him.

Philippians 3:9 [That I] may be found in Him, not having a righteousness of my own derived from *the* Law, but that which is through faith in Christ, the righteousness which *comes* from God on the basis of faith.

Titus 3:4-7

213. Can only a repentant sinner have this faith in Christ?
Yes; the faith which lays hold of Christ and His righteousness can be brought about only in that heart which bitterly feels the pain and misery of living in sin.

> **Matthew 9:12b** [Jesus] said, "*It is* not those who are healthy who need a physician, but those who are sick."
> **Luke 18:9-14**

214. Is true and living faith always and in all persons equally strong?
No; it is often very weak and hardly able to avail itself of the grace of God.

> **Mark 9:24b** "I do believe; help my unbelief."

215. How may we know whether this weak faith is true and living?
The true and living faith is known by an earnest hatred of sin and an eager longing for grace.

> **Romans 7:21-25**

216. Does God accept this weak faith?
Yes, indeed; if only it be true and sincere.

> **Isaiah 42:3a** "A bruised reed He will not break and a dimly burning wick He will not extinguish."

217. What benefit do we have from the true and living faith in Jesus Christ?
By faith we are justified, born anew, sanctified, and finally saved forever.

> **Romans 5:1-2** Therefore, having been justified by faith, we have peace with God through our Lord Jesus Christ, through whom also we have obtained our introduction by faith into this grace in which we stand; and we exult in hope of the glory of God.

218. What is Justification?
Justification is the gracious act of God whereby He for Christ's sake acquits a repentant and believing sinner of his sin and guilt, and looks upon him in Christ as though he had never sinned.

> **II Corinthians 5:21** He made Him who knew no sin *to be* sin on our behalf, so that we might become the righteousness of God in Him.
> **Romans 3:24** Being justified as a gift by His grace through the redemption which is in Christ Jesus.

219. What, then, does the believer receive through justification?
He receives the forgiveness of sins and is adopted as a child of God.

> **Acts 10:43** "Of Him all the prophets bear witness that through His name everyone who believes in Him receives forgiveness of sins."
> **Ephesians 1:7** In Him we have redemption through His blood, the forgiveness of our trespasses, according to the riches of His grace.
> **Galatians 3:26** For you are all sons of God through faith in Christ Jesus.

220. What moves God to forgive sin so freely?
His everlasting love and mercy alone.

> **Ephesians 2:4-5** But God, being rich in mercy, because of His great love with which He loved us, even when we were dead in our transgressions, made us alive together with Christ (by grace you have been saved).

221. For whose sake does God forgive us our sins?

For Christ's sake, who has satisfied for the sins of the whole world by His death on the cross.

> **John 1:29b** "Behold, the Lamb of God who takes away the sin of the world!"

222. To what does the forgiveness of sins lead?

The forgiveness of sins leads to the full enjoyment of the blessed rights which belong to a child of God. It also gives free access to the Father's fellowship and blessing and to the glorious inheritance of eternal life.

> **Psalm 32:1-2** How blessed is he whose transgression is forgiven, whose sin is covered! How blessed is the man to whom the LORD does not impute iniquity, and in whose spirit there is no deceit!
> **Romans 8:17a** And if children, heirs also, heirs of God and fellow heirs with Christ.

223. What is the New Birth?

The New Birth is the gracious work of the Holy Spirit whereby He, through His indwelling in our hearts, renews the image of God in us and thus creates a new spiritual man.

> **II Corinthians 5:17** Therefore if anyone is in Christ, *he is* a new creature; the old things passed away; behold, new things have come.
> **John 1:12-13** But as many as received Him, to them He gave the right to become children of God, *even* to those who believe in His name, who were born, not of blood nor of the will of the flesh nor of the will of man, but of God.

224. What change is brought about in us through the New Birth?

We receive a new heart or a new spiritual life:

In the understanding, a new spiritual light;

In the conscience, real peace and joy;

In the will, a holy desire and a steadfast purpose.

> **Ezekiel 36:26** "Moreover, I will give you a new heart and put a new spirit within you; and I will remove the heart of stone from your flesh and give you a heart of flesh."
> **Ephesians 4:24** And put on the new self, which in *the likeness of* God has been created in righteousness and holiness of the truth.
> **Galatians 5:22-23a** But the fruit of the Spirit is love, joy, peace, patience, kindness, goodness, faithfulness, gentleness, self-control.

225. In what does this new life really consist?
It consists in love to God who first loved us.

> **I John 4:7** Beloved, let us love one another, for love is from God; and everyone who loves is born of God and knows God.
> **I John 4:19** We love, because He first loved us.

226. By what means is the New Birth accomplished?
In little children it is accomplished by water and the Spirit in baptism; but in those who have fallen from the grace of their baptism, also by the Word of God.

> **John 3:5** Jesus answered, "Truly, truly, I say to you, unless one is born of water and the Spirit he cannot enter into the kingdom of God."
> **I Peter 1:23** For you have been born again not of seed which is perishable but imperishable, *that is*, through the living and enduring word of God.

227. Is the New Birth necessary to our salvation?
Yes, indeed. Unless one is born again, he cannot see the kingdom of God. John 3:3

> **John 3:6** "That which is born of the flesh is flesh, and that which is born of the Spirit is spirit."

228. What does the Holy Spirit further work in the believer?
He sanctifies and preserves him.

> **II Thessalonians 2:13** But we should always give thanks to God for you, brethren beloved by the Lord, because God has chosen you from the beginning for salvation through sanctification by the Spirit and faith in the truth.

229. What is Sanctification?

Sanctification is the gracious work of the Holy Spirit whereby He day by day renews the believer more and more after the image of God.

> **Hebrews 10:14 (NKJV)** For by one offering He has perfected forever those who are being sanctified.

230. How is the daily renewal accomplished?

The old man, or sin, is put away more and more, and the new man, or the new spiritual life, appears more and more in all our conduct.

> **Ephesians 4:22-24** That, in reference to your former manner of life, you lay aside the old self, which is being corrupted in accordance with the lusts of deceit, and that you be renewed in the spirit of your mind, and put on the new self, which in *the likeness of* God has been created in righteousness and holiness of the truth.

231. How does this new conduct appear in the daily life of a Christian?

A Christian denies himself, strives against the devil, the world, and his own flesh; he grows in love toward God and man and seeks to do the will of God in all things.

> **Matthew 16:24** Then Jesus said to His disciples, "If anyone wishes to come after Me, he must deny himself, and take up his cross and follow Me."
> **I Corinthians 16:13** Be on the alert, stand firm in the faith, act like men, be strong.
> **I Timothy 6:12** Fight the good fight of faith; take hold of the eternal life to which you were called, and you made the good confession in the presence of many witnesses.

232. Is the believer, then, justified and saved by his own good works?

No; our best works accomplish nothing to this end; we must build our hope of salvation on Christ alone and His righteousness.

Philippians 3:9 [That I] may be found in Him, not having a righteousness of my own derived from *the* Law, but that which is through faith in Christ, the righteousness which *comes* from God on the basis of faith.

233. What is the work of Preservation done by the Holy Spirit?
Preservation is the gracious work of the Holy Spirit whereby He keeps us, through all temptations, in the true and living faith in Jesus until the end.

Philippians 1:6 *For I am* confident of this very thing, that He who began a good work in you will perfect it until the day of Christ Jesus.

234. By what means does the Holy Spirit sanctify and preserve the believer?
By the Word of God and the Lord's Supper.

John 17:17 "Sanctify them in the truth; Your word is truth."

235. How does the Holy Spirit preserve the believer?
He teaches and guides, corrects and comforts him.

John 14:26 "But the Helper, the Holy Spirit, whom the Father will send in My name, He will teach you all things, and bring to your remembrance all that I said to you."

236. What are they called whom the Holy Spirit thus sanctifies and preserves in faith?
They are called Children of God, the Elect of God, Holy and Beloved, Members of the Body of Christ. In a body they make up the holy Christian Church.

I Peter 2:9 But you are A CHOSEN RACE, A royal PRIESTHOOD, A HOLY NATION, A PEOPLE FOR *God's* OWN POSSESSION, so that you may proclaim the excellencies of Him who has called you out of darkness into His marvelous light.

237. What is the holy Christian Church?

The holy Christian Church is the congregation of saints or true believers, where the Word of God is preached and the sacraments are administered according to the ordinance of God.

> **Ephesians 1:1** Paul, an apostle of Christ Jesus by the will of God, to the saints *who are* at Ephesus and who are faithful in Christ Jesus.
> **Acts 2:41-42** So then, those who had received his word were baptized; and that day there were added about three thousand souls. They were continually devoting themselves to the apostles' teaching and to fellowship, to the breaking of bread and to prayer.
> **Ephesians 4:11-12** And He gave some *as* apostles, and some *as* prophets, and some *as* evangelists, and some *as* pastors and teachers, for the equipping of the saints for the work of service, to the building up of the body of Christ.
> **I Corinthians 12:13a** For by one Spirit we were all baptized into one body.
> **I Corinthians 10:16-17** Is not the cup of blessing which we bless a sharing in the blood of Christ? Is not the bread which we break a sharing in the body of Christ? Since there is one bread, we who are many are one body; for we all partake of the one bread.

238. Why is the church called holy?

The church is called holy because of the indwelling of the Holy Spirit, who performs His sanctifying work in all its members. For this reason the church is called holy, in spite of its sins and shortcomings.

239. Why is the church called universal?

The church is called universal because its object is to gather all nations, and because it includes all true believers of all times and all places.

> **Galatians 3:28** There is neither Jew nor Greek, there is neither slave nor free man, there is neither male nor female; for you are all one in Christ Jesus.

240. What is the state of the church on earth?

The church of God on earth is militant.

Matthew 16:17-19 And Jesus said to him, "Blessed are you, Simon Barjona, because flesh and blood did not reveal *this* to you, but My Father who is in heaven. I also say to you that you are Peter, and upon this rock I will build My church; and the gates of Hades will not overpower it. I will give you the keys of the kingdom of heaven; and whatever you bind on earth shall have been bound in heaven, and whatever you loose on earth shall have been loosed in heaven."
Ephesians 6:12 For our struggle is not against flesh and blood, but against the rulers, against the powers, against the world forces of this darkness, against the spiritual *forces* of wickedness in the heavenly *places*.

241. Who are the enemies of the church?
The enemies of the church are the devil, the world, and our own flesh. Its last enemy is death.

I Peter 5:8 Be of sober *spirit*, be on the alert. Your adversary, the devil, prowls around like a roaring lion, seeking someone to devour.
I John 2:15 Do not love the world nor the things in the world. If anyone loves the world, the love of the Father is not in him.
Romans 8:6-7 For the mind set on the flesh is death, but the mind set on the Spirit is life and peace, because the mind set on the flesh is hostile toward God; for it does not subject itself to the law of God, for it is not even able *to do so.*

242. What will be the state of the church in heaven?
It will be triumphant, because all its enemies are conquered.

Revelation 7:9-10 After these things I looked, and behold, a great multitude which no one could count, from every nation and *all* tribes and peoples and tongues, standing before the throne and before the Lamb, clothed in white robes, and palm branches *were* in their hands; and they cry out with a loud voice, saying, "Salvation to our God who sits on the throne, and to the Lamb."

243. Where is the holy Christian church found on earth?
In the congregation, which in the Scriptures is called "the body of Jesus Christ" and "the house of God."

Ephesians 1:22-23 And He put all things in subjection under His feet, and gave Him as head over all things to the church, which is His body, the fullness of Him who fills all in all.

I Corinthians 12:27 Now you are Christ's body, and individually members of it.

I Timothy 3:15b The household of God, which is the church of the living God, the pillar and support of the truth.

I Corinthians 3:16 Do you not know that you are a temple of God and *that* the Spirit of God dwells in you?

Ephesians 2:19-22

244. Are all the members of the organized congregation true Christians?

No; in this organized body, both hypocrites and true Christians are found.

> **Matthew 13:24-30, 47-50**

245. Who are hypocrites?

Hypocrites are those who make outward confession of Christ, but who inwardly and in their conduct deny Him.

> **II Timothy 3:5** Holding to a form of godliness, although they have denied its power; Avoid such men as these.

246. Should the congregation remove these hypocrites from its midst?

Yes; the congregation should expel the openly ungodly and unbelieving, but it cannot judge concerning the secret thoughts of the heart.

> **I Corinthians 5:13b** REMOVE THE WICKED MAN FROM AMONG YOURSELVES.
> **Matthew 18:15-17**

247. Who, then, are true Christians and the real members of the congregation?

They who believe in Christ with all their heart and confess Him both in word and deed.

> **Romans 10:10** For with the heart a person believes, resulting in righteousness, and with the mouth he confesses, resulting in salvation.

248. **What is the intimate fellowship called in which all true Christians live with one another?**

The Communion of Saints.

> **Ephesians 4:4-6** *There is* one body and one Spirit, just as also you were called in one hope of your calling; one Lord, one faith, one baptism, one God and Father of all who is over all and through all and in all.

249. **What precious gift does the Holy Spirit bestow upon us in this Christian church?**

In this Christian church, He daily forgives me and all believers all our sins.

> **Ephesians 1:7** In Him we have redemption through His blood, the forgiveness of our trespasses, according to the riches of His grace.

250. **But does a sanctified person need the forgiveness of sins every day?**

Yes; because sanctification is never perfected in this life, and sin clings to a Christian as long as he is in the world.

> **I John 1:8-9** If we say that we have no sin, we are deceiving ourselves and the truth is not in us. If we confess our sins, He is faithful and righteous to forgive us our sins and to cleanse us from all unrighteousness.

251. **Whom has God given authority to declare the forgiveness of sins?**

The congregation, through its ministers; but any member of the Christian Church may declare it in case of need. (Confession and Absolution)

> **Matthew 18:18** "Truly I say to you, whatever you bind on earth shall have been bound in heaven; and whatever you loose on earth shall have been loosed in heaven."
>
> **John 20:23** "If you forgive the sins of any, *their sins* have been forgiven them; if you retain the *sins* of any, they have been retained."

252. **What is required that a Christian may receive the forgiveness of sins every day?**
That he repents every day, or that he daily feels his sins with deep shame and sorrow, confesses his sins to God, and earnestly seeks the grace of God in Christ.

> **Psalm 32:5** I acknowledged my sin to You, and my iniquity I did not hide; I said, "I will confess my transgressions to the LORD"; and You forgave the guilt of my sin.
> **Colossians 3:5-14**

253. **To whom should a repentant Christian confess his sins?**
First of all to God; then, if he feels the need of it, to his pastor; finally to his neighbor, if he has wronged him in any way.

> **I John 1:9** If we confess our sins, He is faithful and righteous to forgive us our sins and to cleanse us from all unrighteousness.
> **James 5:16** Therefore, confess your sins to one another, and pray for one another so that you may be healed. The effective prayer of a righteous man can accomplish much.

254. **What does the daily forgiveness of sins work in the Christian?**
The daily renewal, or that he day by day becomes more and more thankful to God and increases in childlike obedience and faithfulness.

> **Ephesians 4:23-24** And that you be renewed in the spirit of your mind, and put on the new self, which in *the likeness of* God has been created in righteousness and holiness of the truth.

255. **What becomes of the soul of the believer when he dies?**
His soul goes home to God, where it rests from all strife and sorrow in the blessed fellowship with Him until the resurrection of the body.

> **Luke 23:43** And [Jesus] said to him, "Truly I say to you, today you shall be with Me in Paradise."

Revelation 14:13b "'Blessed are the dead who die in the Lord from now on!'"

Ecclesiastes 12:5b, 7 For man goes to his eternal home while mourners go about in the street. . . . then the dust will return to the earth as it was, and the spirit will return to God who gave it.

256. What is the resurrection of the body?

On the last day, when the Lord Jesus returns to earth, the bodies of the dead shall be made alive and shall be reunited with their souls.

> **John 5:28-29** "Do not marvel at this; for an hour is coming, in which all who are in the tombs will hear His voice, and will come forth; those who did the good *deeds* to a resurrection of life, those who committed the evil *deeds* to a resurrection of judgment."
> **I Corinthians 15:51-52**

257. What change shall then take place in the bodies of the believers?

Their bodies shall arise glorified and incorruptible, like the body of the risen Lord Jesus Christ.

> **I Corinthians 15:42-44a** So also is the resurrection of the dead. It is sown a perishable *body*, it is raised an imperishable *body*; it is sown in dishonor, it is raised in glory; it is sown in weakness, it is raised in power; it is sown a natural body, it is raised a spiritual body.

258. Where do all the risen go after the day of judgment?

The chosen enter into life eternal, the condemned to eternal death.

> **Matthew 25:46** "These will go away into eternal punishment, but the righteous into eternal life."

259. What is eternal life?

Eternal life is the blessed state in which the chosen are free from all evil and live forever in fellowship with their God and Savior, praising God in the company of the holy angels, in everlasting peace and joy.

> **Matthew 25:34** "Then the King will say to those on His right, 'Come, you who are blessed of My Father, inherit the kingdom prepared for you from the foundation of the world.'"

260. What is eternal death?

Eternal death is the dreadful state of separation from God, and everlasting anguish and suffering in hell.

> **Matthew 25:41** "Then He will also say to those on His left, 'Depart from Me, accursed ones, into the eternal fire which has been prepared for the devil and his angels.'"

261. Who are thus condemned?

All who continue in impenitence and unbelief until death.

> **John 3:36** "He who believes in the Son has eternal life; but he who does not obey the Son will not see life, but the wrath of God abides on him."

262. Who, on the other hand, obtain eternal life?

All who continue steadfast in faith until death.

> **Revelation 2:10c** "'Be faithful until death, and I will give you the crown of life.'"

263. Why do you end your confession of faith with the word "Amen"?

Because I know that what I here confess is certainly true.

264. How may you continue steadfast in faith?

By daily asking God to help and strengthen me by His grace.

> **II Peter 3:18** But grow in the grace and knowledge of our Lord and Savior Jesus Christ. To Him *be* the glory, both now and to the day of eternity. Amen.

PART THREE

THE LORD'S PRAYER

265. What is prayer?
Prayer is the childlike communion of our hearts with God in which we tell Him all our needs and earnestly seek some gift from Him.

> **Matthew 7:7-8** "Ask, and it will be given to you; seek, and you will find; knock, and it will be opened to you. For everyone who asks receives, and he who seeks finds, and to him who knocks it will be opened."

266. Who should pray?
All should pray; even little children.

267. But can all pray in this manner?
No, not the impenitent; their hearts are not right with God, and they do not seek Him earnestly.

> **Psalm 66:18** If I regard wickedness in my heart, the Lord will not hear.
> **Isaiah 59:2** But your iniquities have made a separation between you and your God, and your sins have hidden *His* face from you so that He does not hear.
> **Psalm 32:6a** Therefore, let everyone who is godly pray to You in a time when You may be found.

268. In whose name must we pray?
We must pray in the name of Jesus.

> **John 16:23b** "Truly, truly, I say to you, if you ask the Father for anything in My name, He will give it to you."

269. What is meant by praying in the name of Jesus?
To pray in the name of Jesus is to base our prayer on the merit of what He has done for us and His intercession with the Father.

270. How should we pray?

We should pray humbly, confidently as a child, and reverently.

> **II Chronicles 7:14** "And My people who are called by My name humble themselves and pray and seek My face and turn from their wicked ways, then I will hear from heaven, will forgive their sin and will heal their land."
>
> **Hebrews 4:16** Therefore let us draw near with confidence to the throne of grace, so that we may receive mercy and find grace to help in time of need.

271. When should we pray?

The attitude of our hearts should be one of constant prayer, and our communion with God should not be confined to certain times and places, but we should speak with Him whenever we feel the need of it.

> **I Thessalonians 5:17** Pray without ceasing.
>
> **Ephesians 6:18a** With all prayer and petition pray at all times in the Spirit.

272. For whom should we pray?

We should pray not only for ourselves but also for others, even our enemies.

> **James 5:16** Therefore, confess your sins to one another, and pray for one another so that you may be healed. The effective prayer of a righteous man can accomplish much.
>
> **Matthew 5:44** "But I say to you, love your enemies and pray for those who persecute you."
>
> **I Timothy 2:1-3**

273. For what should we pray?

First of all we should pray for the spiritual gifts necessary to our salvation; but we may also pray for other gifts, both spiritual and temporal.

Matthew 6:33 "But seek first His kingdom and His righteousness, and all these things will be added to you."

I Corinthians 12:31a But earnestly desire the greater gifts.

274. **What must we always remember when we pray for things not necessary to our salvation?**
We must always remember that God alone knows whether such a prayer answered would truly benefit us.

When asking for such gifts, we should always add, "Lord, if it is Your will."

Matthew 26:39c "Yet not as I will, but as You will."

275. **Who teaches us to pray rightly?**
The Holy Spirit, who is also called the Spirit of prayer.

Romans 8:26 In the same way the Spirit also helps our weakness; for we do not know how to pray as we should, but the Spirit Himself intercedes for *us* with groanings too deep for words.

276. **Which is the most perfect prayer?**
The most perfect prayer is the Lord's Prayer, which Christ taught His own disciples.

Matthew 6:9-13
Luke 11:1-4

277. **Repeat this prayer.**
Our Father, who art in heaven; hallowed be Thy name; Thy kingdom come; Thy will be done, on earth as it is in heaven; give us this day our daily bread; and forgive us our trespasses, as we forgive those who trespass against us; and lead us not into temptation; but deliver us from evil; for Thine is the kingdom, and the power, and the glory, for ever and ever. Amen.

The Introduction

Our Father, who art in heaven.

What does this mean?

God thereby tenderly encourages us to believe that He is
truly our Father and that we are truly His children, so that we
may boldly and confidently come to Him in prayer, even as
beloved children come to their dear father.

278. **Why would God have us speak to Him as "Our Father"?**
God thereby tenderly encourages us to believe that He is
truly our Father and that we are truly His children, so that we
may boldly and confidently come to Him in prayer, even as
beloved children come to their father.

> **Galatians 4:6** Because you are sons, God has sent forth the Spirit of
> His Son into our hearts, crying, "Abba! Father!"
> **Luke 11:11-13** "Now suppose one of you fathers is asked by his son for
> a fish; he will not give him a snake instead of a fish, will he? Or *if* he is
> asked for an egg, he will not give him a scorpion, will he? If you then,
> being evil, know how to give good gifts to your children, how much
> more will *your* heavenly Father give the Holy Spirit to those who ask
> Him?"
> **Hebrews 4:16** Therefore let us draw near with confidence to the throne
> of grace, so that we may receive mercy and find grace to help in time of
> need.

279. **Who alone can confidently call God "Father"?**
God's children alone can call God their Father.

> **John 1:12** But as many as received Him, to them He gave the right to
> become children of God, *even* to those who believe in His name.

280. Why would God have us say "Our Father" and not only "My Father"?

Because He would have us pray with one another and for one another in spiritual fellowship.

281. What is the importance of the words, "who art in heaven"?

By these words we are reminded of the exalted love and power of our heavenly Father, far above that of any earthly father.

> **Matthew 7:11** "If you then, being evil, know how to give good gifts to your children, how much more will your Father who is in heaven give what is good to those who ask Him!"

THE FIRST PETITION

Hallowed be Thy Name.

What does this mean?

God's Name is indeed holy in itself, but we pray in this petition that it may be hallowed also among us.

How is this done?

When the Word of God is taught in its truth and purity, and we as God's children lead holy lives in accordance with it. This grant us, dear Father in heaven! But whoever teaches and lives otherwise than God's Word teaches profanes the Name of God among us. From this preserve us, heavenly Father!

282. What do you pray for in the first petition?
I pray that the name of God may be hallowed among us.

> **Psalm 72:19** And blessed be His glorious name forever; and may the whole earth be filled with His glory. Amen, and Amen.

283. When is the name of God hallowed among us?
When the Word of God is taught in its truth and purity and is received into our hearts.

> **John 8:31b** "If you continue in My word, *then* you are truly disciples of Mine."

284. When do we hallow the name of God among our fellowmen?
We hallow the name of God when we freely confess it before men, and when we as God's children lead holy lives in accordance with the Word.

> **Matthew 10:32** "Therefore everyone who confesses Me before men, I will also confess him before My Father who is in heaven."
> **Matthew 5:16** "Let your light shine before men in such a way that they may see your good works, and glorify your Father who is in heaven."

285. Who profanes the name of God?
Whoever teaches and lives contrary to the Word of God profanes the name of God.

> **Romans 2:24a** For "THE NAME OF GOD IS BLASPHEMED AMONG THE GENTILES BECAUSE OF YOU."

THE SECOND PETITION

Thy kingdom come.

What does this mean?

The kingdom of God comes indeed of itself without our prayer, but we pray in this petition that it may come also to us.

How is this done?

When our heavenly Father gives us His Holy Spirit, so that by His grace we believe His holy Word and live a godly life here on earth and in heaven forever.

---

286. **What do you pray for in the second petition?**
    I pray that the kingdom of God may come.

287. **What is meant by the kingdom of God for which you pray in this petition?**
    1. The kingdom of grace in which Christ makes every believer a partaker of righteousness, peace, and joy in the Holy Spirit.

       Luke 17:20-21 Now having been questioned by the Pharisees as to when the kingdom of God was coming, He answered them and said, "The kingdom of God is not coming with signs to be observed; nor will they say, 'Look, here *it is*!' or, 'There *it is*!' For behold, the kingdom of God is in your midst."

    2. The kingdom of glory in heaven, where the chosen live with Christ in perfect happiness.

John 14:2-3 "In My Father's house are many dwelling places; if it were not so, I would have told you; for I go to prepare a place for you. If I go and prepare a place for you, I will come again and receive you to Myself, that where I am, *there* you may be also."
Revelation 21:1-4
Revelation 22:1-5

288. **What is meant by saying that the kingdom of God comes to us?**
It means that we become partakers in it.

> **Luke 18:16-17** But Jesus called for them, saying, "Permit the children to come to Me, and do not hinder them, for the kingdom of God belongs to such as these. Truly I say to you, whoever does not receive the kingdom of God like a child will not enter it *at all*."

289. **When does the kingdom of God come to us?**
The kingdom of God comes to us when our heavenly Father gives us His Holy Spirit, so that by His grace we believe the Word of God.

> **John 3:5** Jesus answered, "Truly, truly, I say to you, unless one is born of water and the Spirit he cannot enter into the kingdom of God."
> **Titus 3:5-6** He saved us, not on the basis of deeds which we have done in righteousness, but according to His mercy, by the washing of regeneration and renewing by the Holy Spirit, whom He poured out upon us richly through Jesus Christ our Savior.
> **Matthew 13:1-23**

290. **What does the Holy Spirit work in those who by faith have become partakers in the kingdom of God?**
They live a godly life here on earth and in heaven forever.

> **II Peter 3:13-14** But according to His promise we are looking for new heavens and a new earth, in which righteousness dwells. Therefore, beloved, since you look for these things, be diligent to be found by Him in peace, spotless and blameless.

THE THIRD PETITION

Thy will be done, on earth as it is in heaven.

What does this mean?

The good and gracious will of God is done indeed without our prayer, but we pray in this petition that it may be done also among us.

How is this done?

When God destroys and brings to nothing every evil counsel and purpose of the devil, the world, and our own flesh, which would hinder us from hallowing His Name and prevent the coming of His kingdom; and when He strengthens us and keeps us steadfast in His Word and in faith, even unto our end. This is His good and gracious will.

291. **What do you pray for in the third petition?**
I pray that the will of God may be done among us on earth as it is in heaven.

292. **What is the will of God?**
It is the will of God that all His rational creatures (humans and angels) should praise Him forever in perfect holiness and happiness.

> **Revelation 4:11** "Worthy are You, our Lord and our God, to receive glory and honor and power; for You created all things, and because of Your will they existed, and were created."

293. Where is the will of God done in this manner?
In heaven, where the holy angels praise God in undisturbed peace and joy.

> **Psalm 103:20-21** Bless the LORD, you His angels, mighty in strength, who perform His word, obeying the voice of His word! Bless the LORD, all you His hosts, you who serve Him, doing His will.

294. When is the will of God done among us, as it is in heaven?
When God brings to nothing every evil counsel and purpose that would hinder the hallowing of His name and the coming of His kingdom, and when God strengthens us and keeps us steadfast in His Word and in faith until death.

295. Who seek to prevent the will of God from being done among us?
The devil, the world, and our own flesh. (See Question 241)

296. Who, on the other hand, will help us to do the will of God?
God, who is merciful and faithful, will Himself help us to do His will.

> **I Thessalonians 5:24** Faithful is He who calls you, and He also will bring it to pass.

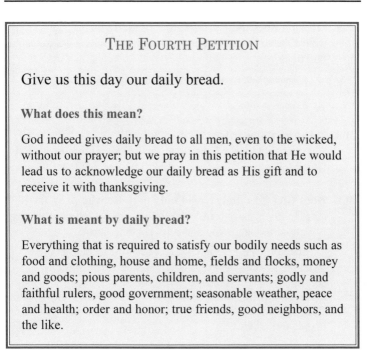

THE FOURTH PETITION

Give us this day our daily bread.

What does this mean?

God indeed gives daily bread to all men, even to the wicked, without our prayer; but we pray in this petition that He would lead us to acknowledge our daily bread as His gift and to receive it with thanksgiving.

What is meant by daily bread?

Everything that is required to satisfy our bodily needs such as food and clothing, house and home, fields and flocks, money and goods; pious parents, children, and servants; godly and faithful rulers, good government; seasonable weather, peace and health; order and honor; true friends, good neighbors, and the like.

297. **What do you pray for in the fourth petition?**
    I pray that God would give us daily bread.

298. **What is meant by daily bread?**
    By daily bread is meant everything that is required to satisfy our bodily needs, such as food and clothing, home and property, etc.

> **Matthew 6:31, 32b** "Do not worry then, saying, 'What will we eat?' or 'What will we drink?' or 'What will we wear for clothing?'. . . For your heavenly Father knows that you need all these things."

299. Of what does the word "daily" remind you?
That I am to be content and satisfied with what God gives me
day by day.

> **I Timothy 6:8** If we have food and covering, with these we shall be
> content.
> **Exodus 16:4-5**

300. Why are the words "this day" added?
They are added that I should not worry about tomorrow, but
let each day bear its own burdens. Matthew 6:34

301. Does God give daily bread only to those who pray for it?
No; He gives daily bread also to the wicked, but they receive
it without thanksgiving and miss His blessing.

> **Matthew 5:45b** "For He causes His sun to rise on *the* evil and *the*
> good, and sends rain on *the* righteous and *the* unrighteous."

302. How should the children of God receive their daily bread?
They should ask God to bless their daily bread and give Him
thanks in return.

> **Psalm 107:1** Oh give thanks to the LORD, for He is good, for His
> lovingkindness is everlasting.
> **Luke 9:16**

**303. Do we need to work for our daily bread since we pray for
it every day?**
Yes; God wants us to be diligent, each in our calling, trusting
in His help.

> **Genesis 3:19a** "By the sweat of your face you will eat bread."
> **II Thessalonians 3:10b** If anyone is not willing to work, then he is not
> to eat, either.

THE FIFTH PETITION

And forgive us our trespasses, as we forgive those
who trespass against us.

What does this mean?

We pray in this petition that our heavenly Father would not
regard our sins nor because of them deny our prayers; for we
neither merit nor are worthy of those things for which we
pray; but that He would grant us all things through grace,
even though we sin daily and deserve nothing but
punishment. And certainly we, on our part, will heartily
forgive and gladly do good to those who may sin against us.

304. **What do you pray for in the fifth petition?**
   I pray that God would forgive us our trespasses.

305. **What is implied by the word "trespasses"?**
   It implies our guilt or debt to God, which we have brought
   upon ourselves by our sins.

> **James 2:10** For whoever keeps the whole law and yet stumbles in one
> *point*, he has become guilty of all.

306. **Can we feel assured that God will forgive us this debt?**
   Yes; Jesus Christ has paid for all our sins.

> **I John 1:9** If we confess our sins, He is faithful and righteous to
> forgive us our sins and to cleanse us from all unrighteousness.
> **I John 2:2** And He Himself is the propitiation for our sins; and not for
> ours only, but also for *those of* the whole world.

307. **Why must the believer ask the forgiveness of sins every day?**

Because he sins every day and is always in need of forgiveness.

> **I John 1:8** If we say that we have no sin, we are deceiving ourselves and the truth is not in us.
> **Romans 7:18-19**

308. **What do we confess to God in this petition?**

We confess that we neither merit nor are worthy of those things for which we pray, but we pray that He would grant us all things through grace.

> **Psalm 130:3-4** If You, Lord, should mark iniquities, O Lord, who could stand? But there is forgiveness with You, that You may be feared.

309. **What do we promise God in this petition, while asking His forgiveness?**

We promise to forgive those who trespass against us and to return good for evil.

> **Luke 6:37b** "And do not condemn, and you will not be condemned; pardon, and you will be pardoned."
> **Colossians 3:13** Bearing with one another, and forgiving each other, whoever has a complaint against anyone; just as the Lord forgave you, so also should you.
> **Matthew 18:23-35**

THE SIXTH PETITION

And lead us not into temptation.

What does this mean?

God indeed tempts no one to sin; but we pray in this petition that God would so guard and preserve us that the devil, the world, and our own flesh may not deceive us nor lead us into error and unbelief, despair, and other great and shameful sins; but that when so tempted, we may finally prevail and gain the victory.

---

310. What do you pray for in this petition?

I pray that God would not lead us into temptation.

311. What is meant by temptation?

By temptation is meant opportunities that invite us to sin.

312. Does God give us such opportunities in order that we may sin?

By no means; God, who is holy and loving, does not tempt anyone to sin.

> **James 1:13** Let no one say when he is tempted, "I am being tempted by God"; for God cannot be tempted by evil, and He Himself does not tempt anyone.

313. Why then does God permit us to be tempted?
God permits us to be tempted in order to try us and in order that it may be seen whether we have true faith, love, and patience.

> **Psalm 66:10** For You have tried us, O God; You have refined us as silver is refined.
> **James 1:12** Blessed is a man who perseveres under trial; for once he has been approved, he will receive the crown of life which *the Lord* has promised to those who love Him.
> **I Peter 1:6-7**
> **Genesis 22:1-19**

314. Who, on the other hand, tempt us to sin?
The devil, the world, and our own flesh tempt us to sin.

315. How does the devil tempt us?
The devil tempts us by putting evil thoughts into our minds.

> **Genesis 3:4-5** The serpent said to the woman, "You surely will not die! For God knows that in the day you eat from it your eyes will be opened, and you will be like God, knowing good and evil."
> **John 8:44c** "Whenever he speaks a lie, he speaks from his own *nature*, for he is a liar and the father of lies."
> **Matthew 4:1-11**

316. How does the world tempt us?
The world tempts us by threats, enticements, and bad examples.

> **Proverbs 1:10** My son, if sinners entice you, do not consent.
> **I Corinthians 15:33** Do not be deceived: "Bad company corrupts good morals."
> **I John 2:16** For all that is in the world, the lust of the flesh and the lust of the eyes and the boastful pride of life, is not from the Father, but is from the world.

317. How does our flesh tempt us?
Our own flesh tempts us by its evil desires.

James 1:14 But each one is tempted when he is carried away and enticed by his own lust.

318. Can we ever be free from temptations in this world?

No; in our earthly life temptations will come, and we need them in order to grow in the kingdom of God.

Matthew 18:7b "For it is inevitable that stumbling blocks come."

Job 23:10 "But He knows the way I take; *when* He has tried me, I shall come forth as gold."

319. What, then, do we mean when we ask God not to lead us into temptation?

We pray that when He finds it good for us to be so tempted, He will guard and keep us so that we may finally prevail and gain the victory.

I Corinthians 10:13 No temptation has overtaken you but such as is common to man; and God is faithful, who will not allow you to be tempted beyond what you are able, but with the temptation will provide the way of escape also, so that you will be able to endure it.

320. How do we guard against temptations?

We must use the Word of God, watch and pray, and take care not to invite temptation.

Matthew 26:41 "Keep watching and praying that you may not enter into temptation; the spirit is willing, but the flesh is weak."

Ephesians 6:13 Therefore, take up the full armor of God, so that you will be able to resist in the evil day, and having done everything, to stand firm.

The Seventh Petition

But deliver us from evil.

What does this mean?

We pray in this petition, in summary, that our heavenly
Father would deliver us from all manner of evil, whether it
affect body or soul, property or reputation, and at last, when
the hour of death shall come, grant us a blessed end and
graciously take us from this world of sorrow to Himself in
heaven.

321. **What do you pray for in the seventh petition?**
     I pray that God would deliver us from evil.

322. **From what evil do we pray God to deliver us in this
     petition?**
     We pray that God would deliver us from all sin that still
     clings to us and from all the destructive effects of sin upon
     soul and body, property and honor.

     > **Romans 7:24-25a** Wretched man that I am! Who will set me free from
     > the body of this death? Thanks be to God through Jesus Christ our Lord!

323. **Can we expect to be entirely free from all evil while in
     this world?**
     No, we cannot; but we pray in this petition that God would
     deliver us more and more from all evil, and that God would
     at last grant us a blessed end and graciously take us from this
     world of sorrow to Himself in heaven.

Philippians 1:23b Having the desire to depart and be with Christ, for *that* is very much better.

THE CONCLUSION

For Thine is the kingdom, and the power, and the glory, for ever and ever. Amen.

What does the word "Amen" mean?

It means that I should be assured that these petitions are acceptable to our heavenly Father and are heard by Him; for He Himself has commanded us to pray in this manner and has promised to hear us. Amen, Amen, that is, Yes, Yes, it shall be so.

324. **What are the closing words of the Lord's Prayer?**
   For Thine is the kingdom, and the power, and the glory, for ever and ever. Amen.

   Revelation 7:12 "Amen, blessing and glory and wisdom and thanksgiving and honor and power and might, *be* to our God forever and ever. Amen."

325. **Of what do these words remind us?**
   We should remember that God is able to answer our prayer, and that the glory belongs to Him alone.

   Psalm 34:3-4 O magnify the LORD with me, and let us exalt His name together. I sought the LORD, and He answered me, and delivered me from all my fears.
   Romans 11:36 For from Him and through Him and to Him are all things. To Him *be* the glory forever. Amen.

326. **What is the meaning of the word "Amen"?**
Its meaning is "Yes, it shall be so."

327. **Why is this word added?**
It is added in order that I may be fully assured that these petitions are acceptable to our Father in heaven and are heard by Him.

328. **How can I feel assured of this?**
God Himself has commanded us to pray and has added this promise to hear us: "Amen, Amen," that is, "Yes, Yes, it shall be so."

> **II Corinthians 1:20** For as many as are the promises of God, in Him they are yes; therefore also through Him is our Amen to the glory of God through us.

329. **Does this promise hold good only when we use the Lord's Prayer?**
No; God hears every prayer offered up according to His will.

> **Matthew 7:7** "Ask, and it will be given to you; seek, and you will find; knock, and it will be opened to you."
> **Psalm 4:3b** The LORD hears when I call to Him.

330. **Does God always answer our prayer as we desire?**
No; He often answers our prayer by giving us something else and something better than we ask or think.

> **Ephesians 3:20** Now to Him who is able to do far more abundantly beyond all that we ask or think, according to the power that works within us.

331. **Does God answer our prayer at once?**
Sometimes; but He often delays His answer in order to
strengthen our faith and our hope.

> **Psalm 27:14** Wait for the LORD; be strong and let your heart take
> courage; yes, wait for the LORD.

332. **In speaking with God, should we only ask for the good
things which we like to get?**
No; we must also return Him thanks for the blessings which
we have received.

> **Ephesians 5:20** Always giving thanks for all things in the name of our
> Lord Jesus Christ to God, even the Father.

THE SACRAMENTS

333. What is a sacrament?
A sacrament is a holy ordinance made by God Himself, in which He gives and confirms His invisible grace through outward and visible means.

334. Which are the sacraments of the Christian church?
They are Baptism and the Lord's Supper.

PART FOUR

THE SACRAMENT OF BAPTISM

335. What is Baptism?
Baptism is not simply water, but it is the water used according to God's command and connected with God's Word.

336. What is God's command concerning Baptism?
It is the word of our Lord Jesus Christ, as recorded in the last chapter of Matthew: "All authority has been given to Me in heaven and on earth. Go therefore and make disciples of all the nations, baptizing them in the name of the Father and the Son and the Holy Spirit, teaching them to observe all that I commanded you; and lo, I am with you always, even to the end of the age."

337. In whose name then are you baptized?
I am baptized in the name of the Father and of the Son and of the Holy Spirit. Matthew 28:19

338. Explain this further.
In Baptism I have entered into fellowship with the Triune God—the Father, the Son, and the Holy Spirit; I have become His own and have been made heir of all His gracious gifts.

> **Colossians 2:12** Having been buried with Him in baptism, in which you were also raised up with Him through faith in the working of God, who raised Him from the dead.

339. Is the Baptism of little children in agreement with Christ's command?
Yes; Christ Himself has said, "Permit the children to come to Me; do not hinder them; for the kingdom of God belongs to such as these" (Mark 10:14).

> **John 3:5** Jesus answered, "Truly, truly, I say to you, unless one is born of water and the Spirit he cannot enter into the kingdom of God."

340. Who should administer Baptism?
Baptism should be administered by the minister of the congregation, but when necessary it may be administered by any Christian.

> **I Corinthians 14:40** But all things must be done properly and in an orderly manner.

341. What benefit do we have from Baptism?

Baptism works the forgiveness of sins, delivers from death and the devil, and gives everlasting salvation to all who believe, as the word and promise of God declare.

Acts 2:38 Peter *said* to them, "Repent, and each of you be baptized in the name of Jesus Christ for the forgiveness of your sins; and you will receive the gift of the Holy Spirit."

Acts 22:16 "'Now why do you delay? Get up and be baptized, and wash away your sins, calling on His name.'"

Romans 6:4 Therefore we have been buried with Him through baptism into death, so that as Christ was raised from the dead through the glory of the Father, so we too might walk in newness of life.

Galatians 3:27 For all of you who were baptized into Christ have clothed yourselves with Christ.

Colossians 2:12 Having been buried with Him in baptism, in which you were also raised up with Him through faith in the working of God, who raised Him from the dead.

Titus 3:5 He saved us, not on the basis of deeds which we have done in righteousness, but according to His mercy, by the washing of regeneration and renewing by the Holy Spirit.

I Peter 3:21 Corresponding to that, baptism now saves you—not the removal of dirt from the flesh, but an appeal to God for a good conscience—through the resurrection of Jesus Christ.

342. What is this word and promise of God?

It is the word of our Lord Jesus Christ, as recorded in the last chapter of Mark: "He who has believed and has been baptized shall be saved; but he who has disbelieved shall be condemned."

343. How does Baptism save us from sin, death, and the devil?
In Baptism we come into fellowship with Christ and are
made partakers in His redemption.

> **Galatians 3:27** For all of you who were baptized into Christ have
> clothed yourselves with Christ.
> **Romans 6:3-4** Or do you not know that all of us who have been
> baptized into Christ Jesus have been baptized into His death? Therefore
> we have been buried with Him through baptism into death, so that as
> Christ was raised from the dead through the glory of the Father, so we
> too might walk in newness of life.

344. How can water do such great things?
It is not the water, indeed, that does such great things,
but the Word of God, connected with the water, and our
faith which relies on that Word of God. For without the
Word of God, it is simply water and no baptism. But
when connected with the Word of God, it is a baptism,
that is, a gracious water of life and a washing of
regeneration in the Holy Spirit, as St. Paul says to
Titus, in the third chapter: "He saved us, not on the
basis of deeds which we have done in righteousness,
but according to His mercy, by the washing of
regeneration and renewing by the Holy Spirit, whom
He poured out upon us richly through Jesus Christ our
Savior, so that being justified by His grace we would
be made heirs according to the hope of eternal life.
This is a trustworthy statement."

345. Why is Baptism called the "washing of regeneration"?
Because in Baptism the Holy Spirit cleanses us from sin and

gives us a new spiritual life.

I Peter 3:21 Corresponding to that, baptism now saves you—not the removal of dirt from the flesh, but an appeal to God for a good conscience—through the resurrection of Jesus Christ.

346. **Is not Baptism also called a covenant?**
Yes; Baptism is a covenant. In Baptism God gives us a new life and His grace, and we promise Him to renounce the devil and all his works and all his ways and to believe in the Father, the Son, and the Holy Spirit.

Colossians 2:11-15

347. **Who enjoy the blessings that God promises in Baptism?**
All who remain in the covenant of their Baptism.

Revelation 2:10c "'Be faithful until death, and I will give you the crown of life.'"

348. **When does the one who was baptized as a child confirm the covenant of his Baptism?**
At his confirmation, when he renews the covenant of his Baptism in the presence of the assembled congregation, having first been instructed in God's Word.

349. **Is it possible to remain in the grace of our Baptism?**
Yes; by the grace of God it is possible.

Philippians 4:13 I can do all things through Him who strengthens me.
Philippians 2:13 For it is God who is at work in you, both to will and to work for *His* good pleasure.

350. **What must we do to remain in the grace of our Baptism?**
We must watch and pray and make diligent use of the Word of God and the Lord's Supper.

I Peter 2:2 Like newborn babies, long for the pure milk of the word, so that by it you may grow in respect to salvation.

351. In what ways may we break the covenant of our Baptism?
1. When we little by little forget our covenant, resist the Holy Spirit, and neglect prayer, so that we become more and more worldly-minded.

2. When we fall into coarse and open sins.

> **I Peter 2:11** Beloved, I urge you as aliens and strangers to abstain from fleshly lusts which wage war against the soul.

352. Will God again receive us when we have broken the covenant of our Baptism?
Yes; God has not broken His part of the covenant, and when we again turn to Him, He is always glad to receive us.

> **Luke 15:20** "So he got up and came to his father. But while he was still a long way off, his father saw him and felt compassion *for him*, and ran and embraced him and kissed him."

353. How does a repentant sinner get courage to return to God?
He gets courage from considering the tender Gospel invitation of Christ and from seeking God in prayer.

> **Matthew 11:28** "Come to Me, all who are weary and heavy-laden, and I will give you rest."

354. Does the one who remains true to the covenant of his Baptism also need repentance?
Yes; he needs daily repentance and daily renewal. (See Question 250)

355. What does such baptizing with water signify?
It signifies that the old Adam in us, together with all sins and evil lusts, should be drowned by daily sorrow and repentance and be put to death; and that the new man should daily come forth and rise to live before God in righteousness and holiness forever.

Romans 6:4 Therefore we have been buried with Him through baptism into death, so that as Christ was raised from the dead through the glory of the Father, so we too might walk in newness of life.

356. What is meant by saying that the old Adam in us should die and the new man appear more and more?
Sin should be rooted out from us through daily sorrow and repentance, and our love to God and man should grow up within us more and more, so that it may appear in all our conduct that we have the mind of Christ.

Ephesians 4:22-24 That, in reference to your former manner of life, you lay aside the old self, which is being corrupted in accordance with the lusts of deceit, and that you be renewed in the spirit of your mind, and put on the new self, which in *the likeness of* God has been created in righteousness and holiness of the truth.

357. What are the duties of sponsors?
They should pray for the child whose Baptism they have witnessed, they should remember the covenant of their own Baptism, and afterwards, as far as possible, see that the child is brought up in the fear of God.

CONFESSION

What is Confession?

Confession consists of two parts: the one is that we confess our sins; the other, that we receive absolution or forgiveness from the pastor as from God Himself, in no way doubting, but firmly believing that our sins are thereby forgiven before God in heaven.

What sins should we confess?

Before God we should acknowledge ourselves guilty of all manner of sins, even those of which we are not aware, as we do in the Lord's Prayer. To the pastor we should confess only those sins which we know and feel in our hearts.

What are such sins?

Here examine yourself in the light of the Ten Commandments, whether as father or mother, son or daughter, master or servant, you have been disobedient, unfaithful, slothful, ill-tempered, unchaste, or quarrelsome, or whether you have injured anyone by word or deed, stolen, neglected or wasted anything, or done any other evil.

Relating to Confession, see also Questions 251-253.

Part Five

THE SACRAMENT OF THE ALTAR

358. What is the Sacrament of the Altar?
It is the true Body and Blood of our Lord Jesus Christ, under the bread and wine, given unto us Christians to eat and to drink, as it was instituted by Christ Himself.

359. What are the words of institution?
"Our Lord Jesus Christ, in the night in which He was betrayed, took bread; and when He had given thanks, He broke it and gave it to His disciples saying, 'Take, eat; this is My Body, which is given for you; this do in remembrance of Me.'

"In the same manner, also, when He had eaten, He took the cup, and when He had given thanks, He gave it to them saying, 'Drink of it, all of you; this cup is the New Testament in My Blood, which is shed for you, and for many, for the forgiveness of sins; this do, as often as you drink it, in remembrance of Me.'"

360. When did Jesus institute the Lord's Supper?
In the night in which He was betrayed to death.

Matthew 26:26-29

361. Is it important to note the time when Jesus instituted the Lord's Supper?

Yes; for it shows the loving care of our Savior, who just
before His suffering and death thought more of us than of
Himself.

John 13:1-5

362. **What do we receive in the Lord's Supper?**
In and with the bread and the wine, we receive the body and
blood of Christ, which He gave up in death for us.

> **I Corinthians 10:16** Is not the cup of blessing which we bless a
> sharing in the blood of Christ? Is not the bread which we break a
> sharing in the body of Christ?

363. **How do you know this?**
Christ says concerning the bread: "Take, eat; this is my
Body."

Concerning the wine He says: "Drink of it, all of you; this
cup is the New Testament in My Blood."

364. **What is meant by "New Testament" in this connection?**
It is the new covenant which God has made and sealed with
the blood of Jesus.

> **Hebrews 9:15** For this reason He is the mediator of a new covenant, so
> that, since a death has taken place for the redemption of the
> transgressions that were *committed* under the first covenant, those who
> have been called may receive the promise of the eternal inheritance.

365. **What, therefore, makes the bread and the wine a
sacrament of the body and blood of Christ?**
God's own Word which is added to the bread and the wine;
for as Luther says, "Bread and wine alone are but bread and
wine; but being united with the Word of God, they are truly
the body and blood of Christ. For as the mouth of Christ
speaks, so it is; He can neither lie nor deceive."

366. For whom is the Lord's Supper intended?
The Lord's Supper is intended for true Christians who are of such age and understanding that they can examine themselves.

> **I Corinthians 11:28** But a man must examine himself, and in so doing he is to eat of the bread and drink of the cup.

---

367. What benefit do we have from the Lord's Supper?
It is pointed out in these words: "Given and shed for you for the forgiveness of sins." Through these words, the forgiveness of sins, life and salvation are given unto us in the Sacrament. For where there is forgiveness of sins, there is also life and salvation.

---

368. But doesn't the believer have the forgiveness of sins before he partakes of the Lord's Supper?
Yes; he does. The believer has the forgiveness of sins through Baptism and the Word.

369. How, then, can the forgiveness of sins be specifically connected with this sacrament?
Because in the Lord's Supper we receive the body and blood of Christ, which were offered up for us, as a sure promise of the forgiveness of sins.

> **Matthew 26:28** "For this is My blood of the covenant, which is poured out for many for forgiveness of sins."

370. In what way does the believer receive life and salvation through this sacrament?
Through this sacrament the believer is brought into spiritual

fellowship with his Lord and Savior, who imparts Himself to him and thus preserves and strengthens him in faith, hope, and love unto eternal life.

> **John 6:56** "He who eats My flesh and drinks My blood abides in Me, and I in him."

371. Does the Sacrament of the Lord's Supper also bring about a more intimate fellowship between believers?
Yes; believers are united in a closer fellowship through partaking in common of the Lord Jesus and eternal life in Him.

> **I Corinthians 10:17** Since there is one bread, we who are many are one body; for we all partake of the one bread.

---

372. How can the bodily eating and drinking produce such great benefits?
The eating and drinking, indeed, do not produce them, but the words: "Given and shed for you for the forgiveness of sins." For besides the bodily eating and drinking, these words are the chief thing in the Sacrament; and anyone who believes them has what they say and declare, namely, the forgiveness of sins.

---

373. Is it important how we receive the Lord's Supper?
Yes; we must be prepared when we go to partake of these gifts. It is much worse to go to the Lord's Supper unprepared and unworthy than not to go at all.

> **I Corinthians 11:27-29** Therefore whoever eats the bread or drinks the cup of the Lord in an unworthy manner, shall be guilty of the body and

the blood of the Lord. But a man must examine himself, and in so doing he is to eat of the bread and drink of the cup. For he who eats and drinks, eats and drinks judgment to himself if he does not judge the body rightly.

---

374. Who, then, receives this Sacrament worthily?
Fasting and bodily preparation are indeed a good outward discipline, but that person is truly worthy and well prepared who believes these words: "Given and shed for you for the forgiveness of sins." But anyone who does not believe these words or who doubts them is unworthy and unprepared, for the words "for you" require truly believing hearts.

---

375. Who, then, is rightly prepared to partake of the Lord's Supper?
He who believes these words: "Given and shed for you for the forgiveness of sins."

> **Psalm 51:17** The sacrifices of God are a broken spirit; a broken and a contrite heart, O God, You will not despise.

376. What is meant by "believing" these words?
This means that we heartily feel our sin and unworthiness before God, but also that we confidently accept for ourselves the grace of our Lord Jesus Christ.

> **Isaiah 55:7a** Let the wicked forsake his way and the unrighteous man his thoughts.
> **Ephesians 2:8** For by grace you have been saved through faith; and that not of yourselves, *it is* the gift of God.

377. **Who partake of the Lord's Supper unworthily?**
They who do not feel nor repent of their sins and who do not from their heart believe in Jesus.

> **I Corinthians 11:29** For he who eats and drinks, eats and drinks judgment to himself if he does not judge the body rightly.

378. **Why do such unconverted persons partake of the Lord's Supper?**
They do so either from custom or habit, or because they are ashamed to neglect the Lord's Supper, or again because they mean to please God by this outward obedience.

> **Isaiah 29:13**

379. **Should such persons be admitted to the Lord's Supper?**
No.

> **Matthew 7:6a** "Do not give what is holy to dogs, and do not throw your pearls before swine."

380. **What must we do in order that we may not partake of the Lord's Supper unworthily?**
We must prayerfully search our own hearts as in the presence of God, whether we repent of our sins and believe in Jesus Christ and whether we have an honest purpose to abstain from even our secret and most cherished sins.

> **I Corinthians 11:28**

381. **How often should we partake of the Lord's Supper?**
Christ has not told us how often we should partake, but He has said, "This do, as often as you drink it, in remembrance of Me."

382. **What should move us to partake of the Lord's Supper often?**

First of all, the command and promise of our Lord and Savior; then, our own great need, which is the reason for our Father's tender invitation and promise of grace.

> **I Timothy 1:15** It is a trustworthy statement, deserving full acceptance, that Christ Jesus came into the world to save sinners, among whom I am foremost *of all.*

383. **What are the common causes for the neglect of the Lord's Supper?**

Spiritual dullness and indifference, a worldly mind, pride, and disregard for God's grace and ordinance.

384. **Should the feeling of our own unworthiness keep us away from the Lord's Supper?**

No; the more we feel our own unworthiness and the more we sincerely long for God's forgiveness, the more worthy we are to receive His grace. (See Question 374)

> **Matthew 5:3** "Blessed are the poor in spirit, for theirs is the kingdom of heaven."
> **I Peter 5:5c** For GOD IS OPPOSED TO THE PROUD, BUT GIVES GRACE TO THE HUMBLE.
> **Psalm 34:18** The LORD is near to the brokenhearted and saves those who are crushed in spirit.

385. **What must we do when we receive the Lord's Supper?**

We must remember our Savior and His death.

> **Luke 22:19** And when He had taken *some* bread *and* given thanks, He broke it and gave it to them, saying, "This is My body which is given for you; do this in remembrance of Me."

386. How should we remember Christ's death?

We should earnestly fix our mind upon the suffering and death of Christ so that we may be strengthened in faith and in love to Him, who loved us unto death.

> **I Corinthians 11:26** For as often as you eat this bread and drink the cup, you proclaim the Lord's death until He comes.

387. What should be our conduct when we have received the Lord's Supper?

We should quietly think of the great love which God has shown us and heartily thank Him for it, not only for a few days, but always. We should keep near to Jesus, show His death in word and act, and in a sanctified life prove that the body and blood of Christ have power to cleanse from sin.

> **I Peter 2:24** And He Himself bore our sins in His body on the cross, so that we might die to sin and live to righteousness; for by His wounds you were healed.

388. Is he who thus believes and lives in fellowship with Christ sure to be saved?

Yes; when he continues steadfast in faith until death.

> **Matthew 24:13** "But the one who endures to the end, he will be saved."
>
> **Revelation 2:10c** "'Be faithful until death, and I will give you the crown of life.'"

Ecumenical Creeds
of the Christian Faith

with introductions by Rev. Jerry Moan

A creed is a confession of faith, a brief statement of beliefs. The word "creed" comes from the Latin word *credo* ("I believe"), which begins both the Apostles' and Nicene Creeds. The creeds of Christianity have served a variety of functions in the church. They were commonly used in connection with baptism and instruction of new Christians. Creeds express what Christians believe about God and His Word. They are also a safeguard for the Church against the threat of false teachings.

Three creeds in particular are referred to as "ecumenical creeds" due to their use by churches around the world: the Apostles' Creed, the Nicene Creed, and the Athanasian Creed. After these had been written, few creeds were added until the Reformation period. Luther underscores how creeds serve as a link with believers of the past: "We fabricate nothing new, but retain, and hold to, the old Word of God as the ancient Church confessed it; hence we are, just like it, the true ancient Church, teaching and believing the same Word of God."[1]

[1] John Theodore Mueller, *Christian Dogmatics* (St. Louis: Concordia Publishing House, 1955), 75.

THE APOSTLES' CREED

The Apostles' Creed holds the place of honor as the best known of all the creeds. Many would be surprised, however, to learn that this creed was almost certainly not written by the apostles themselves. Yet it stands as an ancient summary of the Christian faith, rooted in the teachings of the apostles of our Lord. Martin Luther said of the Apostles' Creed: "Christian truth could not possibly be put into a shorter and clearer statement."[1]

The text as we confess it today dates from the eighth century. It is a revision of what is called the Old Roman Creed which dates back to the second century A.D. In these early centuries, the Apostles' Creed was used as a baptismal confession. It was also used to refute the false teachings of Marcion and groups such as the Gnostics. The Creed's purpose, then, is in no way to take the place of Scripture but rather to summarize the teachings of the Word of God and to protect the church from error.

What do we confess in this creed? First, we express our personal faith in the Triune God of the Bible. We confess that He is the Creator who has provided the only way of salvation for sinners. We are reminded of all that Jesus suffered on our behalf. (Gnostics would have denied that Jesus was born of a virgin or that He could have died a real death.) The Creed further expresses our need for the Holy Spirit's work in our lives. Luther declared, "If one item of this creed is lacking, all items must fall. . . . To be weak in the faith does not do the damage, but to be wrong—that is eternal death."[2] These biblical truths, then, stand as the sure foundation for our faith (Ephesians 2:20).

[1] Martin Luther, *Luther's Works*, eds. Jaroslav J. Pelikan and Helmut T. Lehmann, 55 vols. (St. Louis: Concordia Publishing House/Philadelphia: Fortress Press, 1955-1975), 37:360.

[2] Ewald M. Plass, comp., *What Luther Says: A Practical In-Home Anthology for the Active Christian* (St. Louis: Concordia Publishing House, 1959), 487-488.

I believe in God the Father Almighty, Maker of heaven and earth;

And in Jesus Christ His only Son, our Lord; Who was conceived by the Holy Spirit, Born of the Virgin Mary; Suffered under Pontius Pilate, Was crucified, dead, and buried; He descended into hell; The third day He rose again from the dead; He ascended into heaven, And is seated on the right hand of God the Father Almighty; From where He shall come to judge the living and the dead.

I believe in the Holy Spirit; The holy Christian Church, The Communion of Saints; The Forgiveness of sins; The Resurrection of the body; And the Life everlasting. Amen.

THE NICENE CREED

In the year 325 A.D., the emperor Constantine, troubled by the lack of harmony within the church, convened a church council in the Asian city of Nicaea. A dispute had erupted about the deity of Christ. A teacher from Alexandria, Egypt, named Arius argued that Jesus was actually a created being who did not exist as true God from all eternity. The Council of Nicaea condemned this Arian heresy, reaffirming the scriptural teaching of Christ's full deity and His oneness with the Father. The Bible presents Jesus the Son as true God in every respect, being "of one substance with the Father." Luther called this Nicene Council "the most sacred of all councils."[1]

Present at the Council of Nicaea was a great champion for biblical truth named Athanasius (c.295-373 A.D.). As bishop of Alexandria in Egypt, Athanasius did more than anyone else to see that the orthodox Nicene faith prevailed over Arianism. In fact, he devoted forty-five years of his life to this fight even after being banished by the emperor. This gave rise to the Latin saying: "Athanasius against the world." Athanasius was convinced of the sufficiency of Scripture, even as Luther was centuries later in the Reformation.

Less than a decade after the death of Athanasius, the Council of Constantinople (381 A.D.) expanded the earlier Nicene Creed, affirming the equality of the Holy Spirit with the Father as true God. Through the centuries, this Creed has heralded the scriptural truth about our God and His salvation.

[1] Martin Luther, *Luther's Works*, eds. Jaroslav J. Pelikan and Helmut T. Lehmann, 55 vols. (St. Louis: Concordia Publishing House/Philadelphia: Fortress Press, 1955-1975), 31:318.

I believe in one God, the Father Almighty, Maker of heaven and earth, And of all things visible and invisible.

And in one Lord Jesus Christ, the only-begotten Son of God, Begotten of His Father before all worlds, God of God, Light of Light, Very God of very God, Begotten, not made, Being of one substance with the Father, By whom all things were made: Who for us, and for our salvation, came down from heaven, And was incarnate by the Holy Spirit of the virgin Mary, And was made man; And was crucified also for us under Pontius Pilate. He suffered and was buried; And the third day He rose again according to the Scriptures, And ascended into heaven, And is seated on the right hand of the Father. And He shall come again with glory to judge both the living and the dead: Whose kingdom shall have no end.

And I believe in the Holy Spirit, The Lord and Giver of life, Who proceeds from the Father and the Son, Who with the Father and the Son together is worshiped and glorified, Who spoke by the Prophets. And I believe in one holy Christian and apostolic Church. I acknowledge one Baptism for the remission of sins. And I look for the Resurrection of the dead, And the Life of the world to come. Amen.

THE ATHANASIAN CREED

The Athanasian Creed is named after Athanasius, who was bishop of Alexandria, Egypt, in the fourth century A.D. However, it is almost certain that the Creed was not written by him. Athanasius wrote in Greek while this creed was originally penned in Latin. The Athanasian Creed was probably written by an unknown author either in southern Gaul (France) or northern Africa in the fifth century A.D.

The Athanasian Creed contains a clear statement of the doctrine of the Trinity: there is one God, yet three persons in that one God. The Creed affirms that "the Father is God, the Son is God, and the Holy Spirit is God; and yet there are not three Gods but one God." This Creed also clearly presents the doctrine of the two natures of Christ: Christ is both God and man. The Creed teaches that Christ was not "created, but was begotten by the Father." It further declares that Jesus was fully God and yet true Man, who suffered and died for our salvation, rose again, ascended into heaven, and is coming again "to judge the living and the dead." The Creed affirms that both doctrines are "necessary for our salvation."

Luther regarded the Athanasian Creed as possibly the greatest doctrinal statement of the church since the time of the apostles. In 1537, he wrote about the three Creeds of the Christian faith. Ever since, followers of Luther have shared his appreciation for these ancient restatements of biblical truth.

Whoever wishes to be saved must, above all else, hold the true Christian faith. Whoever does not keep it whole and undefiled will without doubt perish for eternity.

This is the true Christian faith, that we worship one God in three Persons and three Persons in one God without confusing the Persons or dividing the divine substance.

For the Father is one Person, the Son is another, and the Holy Spirit is still another, but there is one Godhead of the Father and of the Son and of the Holy Spirit, equal in glory and coequal in majesty.

What the Father is, that is the Son and that is the Holy Spirit: the Father is uncreated, the Son is uncreated, the Holy Spirit is uncreated; the Father is unlimited, the Son is unlimited, the Holy Spirit is unlimited; the Father is eternal, the Son is eternal, the Holy Spirit is eternal; and yet They are not three Eternals but one Eternal, just as there are not Three Who are uncreated and Who are unlimited, but there is One who is uncreated and unlimited.

Likewise the Father is almighty, the Son is almighty, the Holy Spirit is almighty.

So the Father is God, the Son is God, the Holy Spirit is God, and yet there are not three Gods but one God.

So the Father is Lord, the Son is Lord, the Holy Spirit is Lord, and yet they are not three Lords but one Lord.

For just as we are compelled by Christian truth to acknowledge each Person by Himself to be God and Lord, so we are forbidden by the Christian religion to say that there are three Gods or three Lords.

The Father was neither made nor created nor begotten by anybody.

The Son was not made or created, but was begotten by the Father.

The Holy Spirit was not made or created or begotten, but proceeds from the Father and the Son.

Accordingly there is one Father and not three Fathers, one Son and not three Sons, one Holy Spirit and not three Holy Spirits.

And among these three Persons none is before or after another, none is greater or less than another, but all three Persons are coequal and coeternal, and accordingly, as has been stated above, three Persons are to be worshiped in one Godhead and one God is to be worshiped in three Persons.

Whoever wishes to be saved must think thus about the Trinity.

It is also necessary for eternal salvation that one faithfully believe that our Lord Jesus Christ became man, for this is the right faith, that we believe and confess that our Lord Jesus Christ, the Son of God, is at once God and man:

He is God, begotten before the ages of the substance of the Father, and He is man, born in the world of the substance of His mother, perfect God and perfect man, with reasonable soul and human flesh, equal to the Father with respect to his Godhead and inferior to the Father with respect to His manhood.

Although he is God and man, He is not two Christs but one Christ: one, that is to say, not by changing the Godhead into flesh, but by taking on the humanity into God, one, indeed, not by confusion of substance but by unity in one Person.

For just as the reasonable soul and the flesh are one man, so God and man are one Christ, Who suffered for our salvation, descended into hell, rose from the dead, ascended into heaven, is seated on the right hand of the Father, whence He shall come to judge the living and the dead.

At His coming all men shall rise with their bodies and give an account of their own deeds.

Those who have done good will enter eternal life, and those who have done evil will go into everlasting fire.

This is the true Christian faith. Unless a man believe this firmly and faithfully, he cannot be saved.

Prayers for Various Occasions

Morning Prayers

Now as I awake from sleep,
I thank the Lord who did me keep,
All through the night; and to Him pray
That He may keep me through the day.
All which for Jesus' sake, I say. Amen.

Author Unknown

Jesus, friend of little children,
  Be a friend to me;
Take my hand and ever keep me
  Close to Thee. Amen.

Walter J. Mathams

Father, we thank Thee for the night,
And for the pleasant morning light;
For rest and food and loving care,
And all that makes the world so fair.

Help us to do the things we should,
To be to others kind and good;
In all we do in work or play,
To love Thee better day by day. Amen.

Rebecca J. Weston

EVENING PRAYERS

Now I lay me down to sleep,
I pray Thee, Lord, my soul to keep;
If I should die before I wake,
I pray Thee, Lord, my soul to take. Amen.

18th century bedtime prayer

Jesus, tender Shepherd, hear me,
Bless Thy little lamb tonight;
Through the darkness be Thou near me,
Keep me safe till morning light.

Through this day Thy hand has led me,
And I thank Thee for Thy care;
Thou hast warmed me, clothed and fed me,
Listen to my evening prayer.

Let my sins be all forgiven;
Bless the friends I love so well;
Take me, Lord, at last to heaven,
Happy there with Thee to dwell. Amen.

Mary L. Duncan

PRAYERS BEFORE MEALS

Be present at our table, Lord;
Be here and everywhere adored.
These mercies bless, and grant that we
May feast in Paradise with Thee. Amen.

Isaac Watts

Come, Lord Jesus, be our guest,
And let these gifts to us be blest. Amen.

Traditional

PRAYERS AFTER MEALS

We thank Thee for our daily bread:
Let also, Lord, our souls be fed.
O Bread of Life, from day to day,
Sustain us on our homeward way. Amen.

Author Unknown

God is gracious, God is good,
And we thank Thee for our food. Amen.

Author Unknown

Oh give thanks unto the Lord, for He is good,
For His mercy endures forever. Amen.

from Psalm 107:1

PRAYERS OF PRAISE AND THANKSGIVING

Bless the Lord, O my soul,
And forget none of His benefits;
Who pardons all your iniquities,
Who heals all your diseases;
Who crowns you with lovingkindness and compassion;
Who satisfies your years with good things. Amen.

from Psalm 103

Praise God, from whom all blessings flow;
Praise Him, all creatures here below;
Praise Him above, ye heavenly host;
Praise Father, Son, and Holy Ghost. Amen.

Thomas Ken

THE LORD'S PRAYER

Our Father, who art in heaven,
Hallowed be Thy name.
Thy kingdom come.
Thy will be done, on earth as it is in heaven.
Give us this day our daily bread.
And forgive us our trespasses, as we forgive those who
    trespass against us.
And lead us not into temptation.
But deliver us from evil.
For Thine is the kingdom, and the power, and the glory,
    for ever and ever. Amen.

from Matthew 6:9-13

THE BENEDICTION

The Lord bless us and keep us;
The Lord make His face shine upon us and be gracious unto us;
The Lord lift up His countenance upon us and give us peace. Amen.

from Numbers 6:24-26

GLOSSARY

The aim of this brief glossary is to give the reader a practical and workable knowledge of the most common religious terms found in this book. The following definitions pertain specifically to how these words are used in the text. This is not an exhaustive study; therefore, it will still remain the task of the pastor or teacher to discuss and enlarge upon the definitions wherever necessary.

Absolution 1. God's forgiveness that frees a person from the guilt and punishment of sin. 2. The declaration of God's gracious forgiveness by a minister or another believer.

Abundant More than enough, a plentiful supply, running over.

Abuse Mistreatment, wrong or bad use, vicious conduct, misuse.

Acknowledge To own up to; to admit or confess sin before God and man.

Adam The first man created by God; husband of Eve and the father of the human race.
Old Adam: The old, sinful nature of man; the inborn wickedness of original sin.
New Adam: The new nature given by God through the new birth and indwelling of the Holy Spirit.

Administer To oversee and give out or dispense some benefit, as in offering God's grace in Word and sacrament.

Adultery 1. Sexual intercourse between a married person and anyone to whom he or she is not married. 2. Any unfaithfulness, indecent or impure conduct that violates the marriage. 3. Lustful or impure thoughts, desires, words, or acts in married or unmarried persons.

Altar 1. A structure of wood or stone on which to offer sacrifices to God or to an idol. 2. In the church today, the table or structure at the front of the sanctuary that holds the bread and wine for the Lord's Supper and other articles used during worship.

Anoint To consecrate or set apart someone for ministry (e.g. Christ was anointed by God as Prophet, Priest, and King).

Apostle One of the twelve disciples of Christ, and later the Apostle Paul, all of whom personally met the risen Christ.

Atone 1. To make amends or to make full satisfaction for. 2. Through His death on the cross where, by His body and blood, Christ made full satisfaction for our sin.

Attribute A characteristic or quality of a person that describes what he is like and why he acts as he does. Some attributes of God are His supreme power, holiness, justice, wisdom, kindness, etc.

Authority 1. The right or power to enforce rules or give orders. 2. The person or entity, such as family, church, school, or government, to which that power is given.

Avail Make use of or take advantage of for one's own benefit.

Backbite To speak unkind words behind one's back; to speak evil of a person not present.

Baptism One of the two sacraments in which the Word of God is read and water is applied. The Means of Grace by which a person who is conceived and born in sin becomes a child of God.

Begotten To be the child of. In reference to Jesus, this refers to His relationship as Son to the Father from eternity.

Believer A person who trusts in Jesus Christ as Savior and lives in fellowship with Him.

Blessedness The state in which believers enjoy the love and grace of God who forgives their sin and supplies their needs through Jesus Christ.

Byword Casual use of the name of God or Jesus as a slang expression.

Carnal Refers to man's sinful nature; that which is of the flesh, worldly and sensual; not spiritual.

Chaste 1. Pure in thought, word, and action. 2. Free from sexual impurity such as lust, fornication, and adultery.

Christian A person who has faith in Jesus Christ as Savior and whose life conforms to the teachings of Christ.

Coarse A rough, harsh, or crude manner.

Commandment 1. An authoritative command, order, or law. 2. Any of the ten laws God gave to Moses on Mt. Sinai (Exodus 20:1-17).

Communion (The Lord's Supper) 1. One of the two sacraments in which the Word of God is read and the bread and wine is distributed. The Means of Grace by which a believer receives the forgiveness of sins. 2. The communion of saints is the holy Christian Church where all true believers share in a close relationship with God and one another.

Conceive The beginning of a new life in the womb of the mother.

Condemn To blame and pronounce guilty of a crime.

Confession 1. Admitting one's sin and guilt before God or man (confession of sin). 2. Acknowledging what one believes, as in professing one's faith before others (confession of faith).

Conjure 1. To call on or compel an evil spirit (devil, demon) to cause harm to some person. 2. To seek divine or supernatural help by repeating Scripture or other words as a magic formula to achieve some selfish or harmful result.

Corrupt 1. In a state of decay, tainted. 2. Evil, wicked. 3. Given to bribery, dishonest.

Counsel Advice sought and received in talking with others about what to say or do.

Covenant 1. Covenant of baptism, God's promise of blessing to His faithful children. 2. An agreement between two or more persons.

Covet 1. To eagerly desire something that belongs to another. 2. To desire something that belongs to another person enough to cheat or steal to get it.

Craftiness Skill in deceiving others, slyness, trickery.

Creed A statement of faith expressing basic truths of what we believe about God

Crucify To put to death by fastening to a cross.

Curse 1. To invoke or call down evil upon someone. 2. To swear by using God's name.

Death

Temporal death: End of life in people, animals, or plants in this world.

Spiritual death: Dead in sin and living a life of sin with little or no thought of God; separated from fellowship with God.

Eternal death: Separation from God, the source of life, for all eternity. The devil and all unbelievers in hell are in a state of eternal death.

Defame To harm or damage a person's reputation.

Devil 1. Satan as the prince and ruler of this world and of the kingdom of darkness. 2. Evil spirit, demon.

Devotion 1. Deep, steady affection; loyalty; faithfulness to a person or cause. 2. To study or pray with undivided attention.

Diligent Steady, eager effort in study or work.

Discipline 1. Structured training of the mind or body. 2. Correction for the sake of training or changing behavior.

Dissipation Excessive pursuit of pleasure, including wasteful spending, drunkenness, and gluttony.

Entice To lure a person into some immoral or unlawful activity by appealing to sinful desires.

Estrange 1. To turn a person from affection to indifference or from love to hate; to make unfriendly; to separate or lead astray. 2. To coax or urge a married man or woman to leave their spouse.

Eternity 1. Endless time and existence. 2. The period to follow the end of the world when life will continue forever, whether in heaven or hell.

Evangelist A Christian who preaches the Gospel with the purpose of converting unbelievers or reviving the faith of believers.

Everlasting Eternal, endless, lasting forever.

Faith 1. Trust in or reliance upon Jesus Christ for salvation.
2. A gift of God through which we receive His saving grace.

Fasting To abstain from food, wholly or in part, for a certain period of time. Often connected with prayer as a means of spiritual discipline for repentance or in seeking God's will.

Flesh 1. Our physical body. 2. Our sinful nature that we inherited from Adam. 3. The union between husband and wife referred to in Matthew 19:4-6 ("and the two shall become one flesh").

Fornication Any sexual act between unmarried persons.

Fraud 1. To deceive with the intent of gaining by another's loss, often by cheating or dishonesty. 2. Taking unfair advantage of another in business.

Gluttony Eating or consuming excessive amounts of food or drink.

Grace 1. Unmerited or undeserved love. 2. The attribute of God whereby He desires to save sinners. 3. The favor and mercy of God that comes to us through His Son Jesus Christ, and through His Word.

Hallowed Holy; greatly respected and revered.

Hypocrite Someone whose actions do not conform to what one claims to be.

Impenitence Not being sorry for sin or bad behavior; refusing to repent of sin.

Iniquity Injustice or extreme immorality that is part of our inborn sinful nature.

Jesting Making fun of or mocking in a playful or joking manner.

Justification The gracious act of God by which a sinner, for Christ's sake, is declared righteous, without guilt, and free from condemnation.

Justify 1. Show to be right, fair, or just; to make right. 2. To declare blameless or guiltless.

Kingdom 1. The spiritual rule of God over His people on earth and in heaven. 2. A people or country ruled by a king or queen.

Lust A strong and passionate desire, especially for sexual activity outside of marriage.

Man/Mankind A human being / the human race.

Old man or natural man: The unregenerate, sinful nature that is separated from God by sin, also called the old Adam.

New man or spiritual man: The regenerate nature that is born again by the power of the Holy Spirit, also called the new Adam.

Means of Grace The vehicles or channels through which God gives His grace; namely, the Word of God, Baptism, and the Lord's Supper.

Militant Referring to conflict or war; used to describe the church on earth in the spiritual battle against its enemies.

Nature 1. The inborn character and qualities of a person. 2. A general term given to all creation.

Ordinance 1. A rule or order given by someone in authority. 2. A law or command of God. 3. An established religious ceremony or rite.

Original Sin 1. First sin committed by Adam and Eve which corrupted the human race and is now present in all people from conception. 2. The inborn tendency to disobey God.

Partaker One who shares in something with others and receives a benefit.

Perjury Willfully lying after taking an oath to tell the truth.

Petition A formal request, supplication, or prayer.

Pious Godly, devout.

Pretense 1. Behaving in a way that is not genuine, with the intention of deceiving. 2. A false appearance.

Profane Show contempt or disrespect toward God or anything sacred.

Prophet 1. One who proclaims the word of God. 2. One who tells what will happen in the future. 3. A religious leader.

Redeem 1. To buy back with a price. 2. To rescue from captivity. 3. To rescue from sin and its consequences.

Regard To pay attention, to consider, to take into account.

Regenerate 1. To give new life to what is dead. 2. To be born again of water and the Spirit.

Repentance To recognize, confess, and turn away from sin.

Sabbath The seventh day of the week appointed by God as a day of rest and worship for His Old Testament people. Christians generally observe Sunday as a day of rest and worship, following the pattern of the New Testament believers, because Christ arose from the dead on the first day of the week and the Holy Spirit was given on the first day of the week.

Sacrament A holy ordinance made by God as an outward and visible sign of His inward and invisible grace (Baptism and the Lord's Supper).

Saint 1. A Christian believer in whom the Holy Spirit dwells. 2. All those in heaven who have been redeemed by the blood of Christ.

Salvation Deliverance from the guilt and penalty of sin through the atoning death of Christ.

Sanctify 1. To set apart as holy, belonging to God. 2. To make holy, to purify from sin.

Sin 1. To miss the mark, to fall short of the perfect will of God. 2. Any thought, feeling, word, or act in which we disobey a command of God.

Slander Deceptive or malicious words that damage a person's reputation.

Slothful Lazy, idle, not willing to work.

Superstition 1. An irrational belief based on fear and ignorance. 2. Actions or rituals that people think will bring good luck.

Table of the Law One of the two flat pieces of stone on which God wrote the commandments. The first Table of the Law (commandments 1-3) defines our relationship to God, and the second Table of the Law (commandments 4-10) defines our relationship to other people.

Temporal Temporary; belonging to this world; ending when the world ends.

Tempt To invite or lead someone to do what is wrong.

Transgress 1. To go outside the boundary. 2. To break a law, rule, or moral code.

Trespass 1. To go onto someone's land or property without permission. 2. To sin.

Triune Three in one; describes the Godhead of Father, Son, and Holy Spirit.

Unbelief 1. Absence of belief in God. 2. A refusal to believe. 3. Lack of faith in Jesus Christ as Savior.

Vain 1. Using God's name in a thoughtless or disrespectful manner, as in swearing and cursing. 2. Having no purpose; unproductive, fruitless.

Virgin A pure, unmarried person who has not had sexual intercourse.

Wrath 1. The overwhelming and righteous anger of God against all sin, evil, and unbelief. 2. God's punishment for sin.